The Big Book of Church Humor

The Big Book of Church Humor

More Fun Than Having the Preacher
Over!

Compiled by Ken Alley, P.K.

iUniverse, Inc.
New York Lincoln Shanghai

The Big Book of Church Humor
More Fun Than Having the Preacher Over!

iUniverse, Inc.

For information address:
iUniverse, Inc.
2021 Pine Lake Road, Suite 100
Lincoln, NE 68512
www.iuniverse.com

ISBN: 0-595-29728-5

Printed in the United States of America

Dedicated to my parents,
Joe and Bettye Alley,
Who taught the Christian life by living it…
And laughing a lot.

Introduction

Welcome to THE BIG BOOK OF CHURCH HUMOR! I can't begin to tell you the fun I've had compiling this book. You might recognize some of the guffaws from previous publications of mine, but I decided to put the best of them (plus bunches of new stuff) into one big book.

Book 1 are true stories that I have accumulated from my own memories, personal interviews and e-mails received from doing over 150 radio interviews.

Book 2 are the best fictional anecdotes from past books of church humor, many over 100 years old. They are hilarious and are as appropriate today as they were then because although time goes on, people don't change all that much.

ENJOY!

Ken Alley PK

Copies of this book can be obtained through:
Regular bookstores
On-line bookstores
iUniverse.com
1-877-823-9235

Permissions

All forms of communication are welcome to use individual excerpts from this book as long as credit is given to:

"THE BIG BOOK OF CHURCH HUMOR."

Send ALL your funny stories about ALL aspects of life for future editions and for other books to:

Ken Alley
PO Box 397
York, Ne. 68467
alleykat51@hotmail.com

BOOK 1

Once Upon a Pew

Contents

1

Things Preachers Do and Say

During church announcements one Sunday morning: *"There will be celebration of song at the Immanuel Church in East Rochester. That's the big brown church on Mill St. I can see it from my house. In fact, it's so close I could stand in my driveway and throw a rock and hit that church, that's how close it is."* The announcer turned red, realizing the implications of the analogy, the congregation broke out in laughter.

Our preacher's sermon topic was Samson and Delilah. However, throughout the entire sermon, he kept referring to Samson as *"Tarzan."*

In the middle of a pastor's sermon on the Flood, a sparrow that had gotten in the auditorium the previous day started flying around. The Pastor, not taken aback announced to the congregation that he'd tried to get a dove but the store didn't have any.

A church had recently installed a new central air system. One Sunday it was so hot the air conditioner couldn't keep up. The preacher got up to the podium and apologized, saying, *"I'm sorry it's so stuffy today. We're getting all the B-U-T's into the building that we can."* (BTU's)

In the adult Bible class, our pastor said, *"I'd like to pick everybody's nose this morning…I mean everybody's brain."*

Last week a pastor stood at the pulpit and said, *"I'm going to talk awhile before I say anything."*

Church services were running late and our pastor quipped, *"I'm glad no one is 'clock-eyed' in here."*

The pastor announced, *"The 2:00 service will be held at the rest room."* (Instead of rest home.)

An associate pastor at a Presbyterian church in Nebraska for four years recently moved to Washington state, and at her installation there, the presiding pastor indicated, *"Janine has served time in Nebraska."*

In a sermon at Florence Presbyterian Church, the Rev. Paul Cook admonished the congregation that the prohibition against telling falsehoods was *"the most important commandment."* After a moment's thought, he qualified the statement, *"Well, maybe it's not the most important, but it's right up there with the top ten."*

One time a minister was preaching hot and heavy about Samson. He told about Samson's adulterous affair, about his eyes being plucked out, etc. Then to make his point, he intended to use the phrase, *"beast of burden."* However, somehow he got his syllables mixed up and said, *"They made him a burst of burden!"* *"A beast of beaden!"* by this time, the entire congregation was in an uproar. The minister sighed and said, *"Oh well, he was a strong man."*

A Pastor was giving an informal talk about "Love" at the adult Bible class. Hands thrust in his pants pockets, he paced at the front of the room, and would sometimes unconsciously swing his hips forward when he wanted to emphasize the word "love." After class he received an anonymous note stating that his fly had been down, and his boxers were visible whenever he emphasized the word "love."

Our pastor made this announcement: *"Good news for the family of Roger W. He has had a heart attack…but it's not as serious as first thought."*

A minister was leading a service in a small town in northern Indiana, where the former Republican governor of the state was a regular churchgoer. That mornings topic was the story of the Publican and the Pharisee. But out of minister's mouth the famous Scripture passage came, *"But the Republican would not so much as lift is eyes up unto heaven."*

One preacher said, *"Today's sermon is 'The Quickest Way to Hell!' Let's pause and ask the Lord to guide us."*

While discussing Moses and the episode with the burning bush, our discussion leader read, *"And God said, 'Moses, you're on holy ground, take off your feet.'"*

During the prayers for congregation members, the congregation was asked to pray for Bill W., who was awaiting the results of his biopsy. The pastor actually ended up praying that the results of Bill's "autopsy" would be favorable.

A pastor was commenting on the wonders of our world made by God and told his congregation, *"I saw a beautiful sunset this morning."*

Our pastor meant to say, *"We all know what a tough job child-rearing can be."* What came out of his mouth was, *"We all know how tough child-bearing can be."* What a difference a letter can make!

Another preacher spoke about the *"children of Israel and the Tabelnacker."*

Our minister, preaching out of 1 Timothy, said, *"She shall be 'shaved' in child-bearing."* (Instead of 'safe'.)

"We offer prayers of thanksgiving on behalf of Jeremy W., who has been experiencing health problems. He has undergone a recent brain scan, and they didn't find anything."

The pastor was praying for an elderly lady in our congregation, who had taken a bad fall and was in the hospital. She had fallen down a flight of 14 stairs, but when Pastor was praying for her, he said that she'd fallen down 14 <u>flights</u> of stairs. My husband got one of those cases of inappropriate giggles when he pictured someone falling down 14 flights of stairs like a cartoon character.

A Pastor was preaching one Sunday morning using an illustration about geese. He said that the reason that they fly in a V-formation, is that they can fly for a much greater distance. The reason that they are able to do this is that the goose in front is breaking the wind off the rest of the flock and it is easier for the rest of the flock to fly. Then every once in a while they will change places and the goose in the front of the flock will move to the back and the next one in line will move up and take his turn in the front, braking the wind for the rest. Therefore the ones in the back of the flock can rest.

As he was getting carried away with his sermon he said, *"And I'm kind of tired of being the only one around here that is breaking wind."* And with that, the whole congregation burst out in laughter, so much so that the pastor finally had to dismiss the rest of the service.

An elderly dean of a Christian college was addressing the student body about living the life of a Christian. He compared their lives to life of John in the New Testament. He said, *"We need more Johns around here!"* Everybody became uncorked, but the old fellow didn't have a clue.

The pastor of a church was young and on fire for the Lord. He was a tremendous speaker with powerful messages every week. He was calling on the local church to be a vital part of the community. He meant to say that Grace Bible Church should be an outpost and a lighthouse in our town. Instead, he said that Grace Bible Church should be a light-post and an out-house in our town. On the way out of church a parishioner asked the pastor what he meant by the church being an out-house. He answered, *"I'd hoped no one caught that."*

The message was taken from Romans 6:23. "For the wages of sin is death, BUT the gift of God is eternal life…" Pastor said that passage contained one of the most significant buts in the Bible. Of course, we all heard "The most significant BUTTS in the bible."

Time after time a well-meaning preacher would pray publicly, *"Lord, be with those who are sick of us."* Finally someone took him aside and suggested that he pray, *"Be with those who are sick among us."*

Speaking on communication between husbands and wives, the preacher said, *"Husbands come home at the end of the day and want peace and quiet, while the wife needs to talk with him. All she's heard all day is "ga ga, doo, doo."* (instead of da, da, goo, goo.) He stopped, looked startled, realized his mistake and said, *"Oh well, they say that too."*

A lawyer-preacher leading a prayer before the sermon, made routine opening remarks. As he started on a special plea, he began, *"Your Honor,"* instead of *"Dear God."*

I heard of a preacher who was unable to climb out of the baptistry because he flooded his waders while bending over to lift a new convert up from the water.

While in a Bible class, the minister *announced "Tonight's lesson is, Money Doesn't Buy Happiness."* Having been unemployed for some time, one of the parishioners thought out loud, "No, but it sure makes your misery more tolerable." The preacher replied, *"Son, you just ruined my whole lesson."*

As I awoke during a sermon the pastor said, *"Where the scriptures speak, we speak. Where the scriptures are silent, we sleep."*

While studying the intricate dress of the priests in the Old Testament, the preacher came to the part that describes how the priests put bells on the bottom of their robes. He asked *"Why do you suppose the priests had to tinkle?"* After a second of silence, the class broke up with laughter.

A young preacher still in Bible college was invited to preach to a small downhome congregation during spring break. He chose to preach on "Consistency." All went well until he began speaking about proper dress. He said, *"You Christian ladies wouldn't think about parading around in a mini skirt, yet some of you think it's fine to play tennis in skirts that go all the way up to your _____!"* Fortunately, he caught myself in time to say, *"Well, you know where they go to."*

In Kansas, many preachers are also farmers and ranchers. During one sermon, a preacher-rancher was so preoccupied with the new pickup truck he was buying the next day, he said "pickup" for no reason in the middle of his sermon. He returned to the scriptures after it dawned on him what he had done. Needless to say, he was a little embarrassed, not to mention his wife.

An elder, presenting a young woman who needed money for her summer mission work, referred to her recent employment as a candy stripper (instead of striper).

The preacher was trying to explain where a certain place was located, as he said, *"Not even God knows where this place is."*

Instead of saying the prodigal son ate, *"with the hogs"*, the minister said the prodigal son ate *"like a hog."*

The preacher, walking slowly up to the podium, said, *"Woke up with a nag this morning."* What he meant was, he woke up with a nagging back ache, but the congregation cut loose.

The preacher changed his topic midway through his sermon and didn't know it until someone told him later. The funny thing is, the preacher's wife didn't notice!

While describing the newest addition to a family, the preacher said, *"The baby weighed 18 pounds and was 7 inches long."*

The lesson topic was earthly possessions and how individuals put too much value on them. The minister was listing some of these possessions, such as money, fancy homes, recreational toys, and even living possessions such as pets. He said, *"Yes, even our pets can sometimes have more value than they should. But what am I talking about, when I sleep with a dog!"* Suddenly there was a heavy silence. He thought to himself, "I wonder if anyone thinks I was referring to my wife?" He cautiously looked across the room and there were a couple of people holding in some pretty explosive laughs. He quickly said, *"No, No, I don't mean my wife, I mean Jo Jo, our dog!"* Too late.

The sermon was about throwing all your alcoholic beverages into the river. The next song was "Shall we Gather at the River?"

While talking about parents letting go of the apron strings, the speaker said, "overproductive parents," instead of "overprotective" parents.

Twin sisters were placing membership at a local church and they were introduced as the "sin twisters."

Trying to be creative, a minister started "advertising" his next sermon on the Second Coming of Christ. He had little signs taped on doors, ceilings, the sidewalk, etc., that said, "He's Coming!" In his enthusiasm, he got a clever idea of sending every family of the congregation a note which had no return address that simply said, "He's Coming!" He thought all he had to do on Sunday was step into the pulpit and say, *"In case you haven't heard, He's coming!"* It lost its effectiveness when one of the widows became concerned and call the police.

With a sermon on "Some Things for a Christian to Remember," on his mind, the preacher turned on the water to fill the baptistery, which was directly behind the pulpit. Turning it on and off required a trip downstairs to the other end of the building, and it had no overflow valve. As he began, "This morning I want you to remember…" he heard the splashing of the water behind me. Immediately it dawned on him what he'd done. "Oh, no, I didn't remember to turn off the water in the baptistery! Someone turn it off, quick!," he shouted. Some believed he had planned the whole thing.

The preacher was speaking about how we view sin. He said, *"We look at it, we tolerate it, then we embrace it."* He used an illustration about a woman who was an alcoholic. She was visiting a friend that had left a bottle of wine on the table. The friend had to answer the phone in another room, and while she was gone, the alcoholic became very nervous. She decided to take the cork out of the bottle and just smell the wine. That caused her so much stress that she jumped up and started walking back and forth in the room trying to get her composure. When the preacher got to the point where she walked back and forth, he said, *"She walked up and forth, down and around."* After the service, one of the brethren said to the preacher, *"I thought I would have to get you a road map to get that lady straightened out."*

The shortest prayer ever spoken by a preacher was, *"Dear God, you know our thoughts, Amen."*

During a panel discussion about how important preacher's wives were in their husband's ministries, one preacher said, *"Any woman who wants to be a preacher's wife should be committed."* After a short pause he rephrased that, *"should be dedicated."*

Arriving at the grave sight, the minister began reciting the 23rd Psalm. A dear friend, there to assist him, began his prayer… *"Will you prease play with me?"*, uh uh, *"will you play with me prease?"*, uh uh *"Bow your heads."*

One of our Elders died and the minister was trying to convey the thought that those of us who are younger owe a great debt to the older soldiers who have "Blazed the Trail." He said, *"who have traized the blails," "trailed the blaze,"* then finally *"blailed the trazes."* Whereupon the minister went on to something he could pronounce, like the benediction.

At a funeral where the priest was delivering the eulogy he went on and on about how good the deceased was, what a terrific mother, whose kids were always clean and so well behaved, etc., etc. The only problem was, the deceased had no children.

A Christmas service started with the youth minister and some of the children singing carols. While delivering the sermon, which was about the birth, death, and resurrection of Christ, the minister came to the baptism of Jesus and said ever so sincerely, *"...and the Holy Spirit descended from heaven in the form of a tur-tledove..."* (instead of a dove.) He promptly realized his "blooper," and decided to finish it with a bang and said, *"No, make that two turtledoves and a partridge in a pear tree!"*

Once, while presiding over a funeral, the minister announced that the deceased, *"died of...death."*

A Country Western-loving Elder was a song director. One Sunday morning as he introduced a deacon to lead the prayer he said, *"After the singing of this song, we'll be led in prayer by 'Little Jimmy Dickens'."*

Overheard in a service... *"Will you bow with me as we start the show, I mean the service."*

While preaching on James 3:4, "Behold also the ships, which though they be so great, and are driven of fierce winds, yet are they turned about with a very small helm." The minister wanted to use an "updated" word for the King James version rendering of helm. What he wanted to say was "rudder," but what came out was "udder," which has quite a different meaning. After the services, one of the members who got a chuckle out of the "Blooper," said that his sermon was an "udder" catastrophe.

As a nervous young preacher, slightly unprepared, the minister referred to Matt., 11:16. As he preached, referring to Jesus causing the lepers to be cleansed as one of his miracles, he called them "leapers," much to the delight of the crowd!

A church was between pastors and the interim pastor was a rather pompous old fellow, much given to theatrics. One Sunday morning as the ushers were preparing to bring the collection plates forward, the old reverend came to the front of the platform and intoned, *"Ask and ye shall be given; seek and ye shall find; knock and it shall be opened unto you."* Then he spread his arms wide and shouted, *"Therefore, come unto the Lord, all ye askers, seekers, and knockers."* Needless to say, most of the congregation (with the possible exception of the elderly) were totally wasted for the rest of the service.

At an annual Bible Lectureship at the Christian college, a young and dynamic preacher was given the assignment to speak on the values of attending the mid-week meeting at church. He did a fine job with his lecture. However, the congregation had a hard time keeping straight faces when he got his tongue tangled up and started talking about the values of attending the "mid-meek weeting."

One of the worst blizzards of the year hit one Sunday morning. The minister certainly didn't expect anyone to show up for church. Low and behold, one farmer trudged his way to the front door of the church and came in and sat down. Well, by golly, since he went to all the trouble to come to church, the minister was going to give him his sermon, in all its splendor. After he was finished he said, *"Thanks for the sermon pastor, but you know if I just had one cow come home, I'd feed her, but I wouldn't give her the whole bale of hay.*

One elder of the Church was introducing the guest speaker and he said that he was from *"Corpus Chrispi, Texas."*

The preacher was talking about the women of the Old Testament and remarked about the number of children some of them had. He said some of them were real *"Fertile Myrtles."*

The pastor was talking about Simon Peter and his relationship with Jesus when without realizing it, referred to him as *"Simple Simon."*

A parishioner was listening to a sermon when the Pastor said, *"My God, My God, why hast thou forsooken me?"*

A preacher was talking about how married couples should avoid lumping household tasks into "men" chores and "women" chores. He said, *"After all, most women can rake a lawn, and guys, anyone is capable of using a bust duster."* We think he meant "dust buster,' but maybe there's some new chore we've never heard of!

One Sunday as the pastor was praying for the sick of our congregation, it came time to be more specific, he said, *"And God, especially be with…uh…uh…uh…you know who I mean."* He had forgotten their names.

There was a preacher who left the church and opened up a tobacco store and called it, "HOLY SMOKES".

I heard a burned our preacher say, *"I love the Church, it's the brethren I can't stand!"*

A follower was listening to a sermon once and heard the preacher say that "Jesus was revived," instead of resurrected.

A preacher was announcing the names of people who were on the prayer list. He mentioned that one lady will be entering the hospital that week for a "vasectomy," (instead of a hysterectomy). It was after the services when he became aware of his blooper.

A parishioner was listening to a sermon that made reference to ball players and the preacher referred to Michael Jordan as Michael Jackson.

The preacher was so engrossed in his presentation concerning the crucifixion of Jesus that he said, *"And Mary looked up at Jesus and said, "My God, My God, why hast thou forsaken me?"* Then he said, *"I'm sorry, Mary didn't say that, Jesus did. I mean Jesus said that to God."* He started over.

A pastor remarked that he fell asleep listening to a tape of his own sermon.

How about the preacher who exhorted so fervently about the "fiery darts" of Satan, that he reversed the "f" and "d".

Not knowing exactly how to say "Jesus rode into Jerusalem on his ass," the preacher got twisted and said, *"Jesus rode into Jerusalem on his donkey's ass."*

A church member remarked that she had heard of a preacher referring to the Cross as the "Big T," and Jesus and his apostles as "JC and the Boys."

From the alter in a revival, our evangelist asked that all Christians come forward and pray with the "Seekers." He meant to say, "except for those who have a baby in their lap," or "are holding one in their arms," but he confusingly said, "Unless you are having a baby."

One of the best "Bloopers" ever heard occurred one Sunday when a rather pompous and very "impressed with himself" minister was giving a memory story. He meant to say, "Back when I was a child," but he actually said, *"Back when I was God!"* It was a beautiful Freudian slip that fit the man perfectly. It was also on a live radio broadcast.

At a church picnic, a member was asked by the pastor, who loved to eat, if she had brought her famous coconut cream pie (the pastor's favorite.) She told him no, that she hadn't had time to make one. He replied, *"That's OK, I still love you. Not as much, but I still love you."* She wasn't sure, but she thinks he was serious.

A few years ago, a minister was asked to be a guest speaker at a neighboring church. He met with the liturgist in the Pastor's study, put on his robe, and with much dignity, took his place at the front of the sanctuary. When it came time for him to read the scriptures, he stood and flipped his mike cord out of the way and walked to the lectern. Halfway there, his left leg refused to come along because the cord did a half-hitch around his ankle. It was too late to act as if nothing had happened, so he very carefully removed the obstacle.

Since this act was definitely not in the order of worship, he said, *"It is very evident to me you folks have a line on the preacher."*

While attending a funeral of a friend, a pastor asked the mourners to bow in silent prayer and consider their own morality.

One preacher said, *"I wish I had a pornographic memory to help me remember the scriptures better."*

A woman's husband was preaching one Sunday and instead of saying how their lives shine brightly, he said, "shinely brights."

On a live television interview, the subject was about forgiveness, and the text was Roman's 3:23, "...for all have sinned and fall short of the glory of God." One of the panel said, *"Thanks be to God that delivers us from our falling shorts."*

A pastor was delighted that his small congregation was growing and encouraged members to invite their neighbors to church. One morning, his exuberance got the better of him. Having just toured the newly renovated nursery, he spoke about it from the pulpit, going into great detail about its large size and amenities.

"I'm concerned that it isn't full," he concluded. *"So, what I'd like for all of you to do this afternoon is to get together with your neighbors and work on filling the nursery."*—Contributed by Bill R. Wise, Reprinted with permission from the November 1992 Reader's Digest.

On Mother's Day one pastor said, *"Today we are not only going to honor the oldest mother and the youngest mother, but every single mother."*

The sermon was about counting your blessings. The preacher said, *"Don't ever wish your wife away."* What he meant to say was, *"Don't ever wish your life away."*

The pastor was talking about the church in Anchor, Anchorage. What he meant to say was Anchorage, Alaska.

While preaching a "fire and brimstone" sermon, and getting used to his first set of dentures at the same time...they fell out.

A church member was listening to a sermon when the pastor said something about how cold the weather was, and he said *"The low dippy down to around 30."*

A pastor was talking about the three Presidential candidates "ducking" it out...instead of "duking" it out.

A pastor always enjoyed visits from the members of the congregation. One evening, when he had been feeling under the weather, a family stopped by to chat. A few days later they came over again. In expressing thanks for the previous visit, he said, *"You don't know how I felt when you people left the other night!"*—Robert J. Pietraszek, reprinted with permission from the Nov. 1990 Reader's Digest.

One Sunday morning, the minister asked members to stay after the service so he could pick their brains about an upcoming event. He was quick to add, *"It should only take a minute."*—Melody Rebenstorf, reprinted with permission from the Oct. 1990 Reader's Digest.

In the course of her sermon, the minister referred to the Old Testament story of Balaam and his talking donkey. He explained that God made the donkey talk, and he added *"The donkey was God's 'Better Business Burro'."*

A man's father was giving a lesson prayer. He was also taking the opportunity to explain how to use the concordance in the back of the Bible.

He explained that a person could look up a word and would be given a list of scriptures where the word appears. He told the audience that the list would also include a phrase containing the word, but the word would be abbreviated to only the first letter. Then he gave this example: "Here in the concordance under the heading 'pray' we find this scripture. *'If anyone has troubles, let him p...'.*" (How about p...without ceasing.)

While introducing a new member to the congregation, the preacher said…*"This is Patty _____. She looks just like her older sister who is already a member her, only a smaller virgin."*

All winter long the church roof leaked. Members had to strategically avoid the unwanted water when choosing their seats. Spring finally came and the roof was repaired except for the overhang above the entry way.

One Sunday the entire church was full and some latecomers were standing by the front door looking for a place to sit.

The Pastor said, *"It's wonderful seeing everyone here today. Except for a few drips by the front door, we're ready for a great year!"*

After seeing the collection totals for the month, the pastor said that he wished the government would quit printing $1 bills.

A preacher was talking about traveling on the train and said "AMWAY" train instead of "AMTRAK".

A minister, in the middle of a marriage ceremony, backed up two steps and fell into the floor level baptistry. (Splish, splash, I was taking a bath…)

At the Kevin Hamm and Michele Egging wedding, the preacher said, "We are not only joining two fine young people in matrimony, but we are also joining two fine families, the Hamm and Egg…ing families."

The first time the new minister stepped into the pulpit, he had just opened his mouth to say the very first word of his sermon when there was a brilliant flash of lightning, a deafening roll of thunder, and the power went out. You could say he was a bit intimidated.

In the pastor's opening remarks last Sunday, he said that every day is a new day: "We all make decisions from the moment we get up. We decide whether to have breakfast or not. We decide what shoes to wear. We decide whether to wear pants or a skirt—well, women can decide that anyway—because most men don't wear skirts…at least those who belong to this church…I hope. I, um, probably should continue with my sermon before I get into more trouble."

My daddy tells of the time when the preacher was sternly and loudly declaiming the evils of alcohol. For support he called on a lady who was a pillar of the congregation. "Don't you agree, Sister Anne?" he exclaimed.
"Oh, actually I enjoy a little toddy once in a while," came the quiet reply of the elderly saint.

My pastor was talking about all the years Enoch lived but kept referring to him as a "Eunuch."

Our pastor was leading a serious discussion when his miscue lightened the mood. He said, "As for me, I will serve man, not God."

The pastor's wife fell asleep in the middle of her husband's sermon. Her head rolled back and her mouth opened wide, causing her jaws to lock. The preacher had to stop what he was doing to help his wife shut her mouth.

My father, a retired pastor was visiting from out of state. He was having a "grandfatherly" time with my little ones, playing catch, reading them stories, tucking them into bed. We were all really glad to see him. On Sunday we went to church and he was asked to lead the congregation in the Lord's Prayer. He ascended to the pulpit and asked all to bow their heads and join him in this prayer. He started off, "Now I lay me down to sleep, I pray the Lord my soul to keep…" Everyone laughed, but understood his absentmindedness.

During the sermon our pastor was telling a story where one character quite forcefully tells another to *"SIT DOWN!"* As the preacher shouted these words, he startled an elderly lady at the back of the church who had just stood up, presumably to go out to the ladies' room.

Pastor's sermon was about humility. At the end he asked for those in need to humiliate themselves before the alter.

While talking about the robes that pastors in various denominations wear, one clergy said, *"And some don't wear anything at all."*

My brother-in-law is a pastor who procrastinates worse than any person I know. He types his own bulletins and prints them himself, sometimes as late as one hour before services. One Sunday as he threw the bulletin together, instead of listing the sermon title as, "He Who Sows," he inadvertently typed, "Hey You Sows." It was a tough service to get through.

Pastor was being cool and asked for everyone in the church to turn around and shake hands with the person directly behind them. This was impossible because the person directly behind *you* was facing toward the back, looking for the person directly behind *them*. It was really funny because no one had anyone to shake hands with. (Now if you were supposed to "goose" the person behind you, that would have worked fine!)

My pastor husband stood in front of the congregation and fervently said, *"Let everything that has breasts praise the Lord."* (Instead of "breath.")

My pastor is a very big man who loves the Lord but hates suspenders. He hikes his britches up over his tremendous belly and cinches his belt as tight as he can. In the middle of one of his fire and brimstone sermons he reached his hands to the sky and shouted, "Praise the Lord!" right as his pants fell to the floor. I'll never look at him quite the same.

The pastor announced, *"The Practicing Alcoholics Group will meet after services."* (Instead of "recovering.")

As a pastor in my first church I made a hospital call on a gentleman who, because of severe circulatory problems, had both of his legs surgically removed. I took a young seminary student with me to show him how this type of visitation was done. At the end of the visit as we pleaded to the Lord, I prayed, "Lord, as the Great Physician, will you minister to Mr. Jones so that he might be able to return to his home and get back on his feet." As we left the hospital my seminary friend very respectfully asked me if I realized what I had prayed.

My pastor was preaching about making "certain decisions" and he said "circum...cisions" by mistake.

I was driving home from church one Sunday and listening to a radio preacher announce his sermon title, "OBEY GOD'S COMMANDMENTS" Didn't Moses preach that one?

A preacher gave the following announcement, *"Don't forget the potluck after services. My wife, Marilyn, is bringing her home-baked breads. I just LOVE her buns!"*

About 50 years ago in my previous parish, I had to type stencils and print the bulletins because I didn't have a secretary. A young lady by the name of Daisy, quite active in the parish, would help me from time to time. She was quite well proportioned above the hips and below the shoulders. While thanking her in the bulletin, instead of typing "Daisy," my non-professional script read, "DAIRY." I never did live that one down.

One pastor said, *"Larry Anderson had an emergency episiotomy last night (appendectomy)."*

Instead of welcoming the visitors to *"feel a part"* of the congregation, the pastor inadvertently welcomed them to *"peel a fart."*

The preacher's sermon was a little politically motivated because he kept reminding his congregation to vote against *"Preparation H."* (Proposition).

One Sunday the preacher announced, *"Please turn over in your hymnals."*

One Southern preacher asked the janitor if he had any light "bubs."

As the preacher closed his sermon he asked for anyone in need to come to the front for prayer. An elderly lady slowly made her way down the center aisle. As she poked along the preacher praised her for her commitment to Jesus and how we should all rededicate our lives…right up to the moment she went into the ladies' room, which was located next to the pulpit.

My pastor preached, *"…and a man shall conceive and bear a child."*

The visiting preacher just had to have a cigarette before he gave his sermon, so he snuck into the furnace room where no one would see him. The furnace kicked on and blew smoke all through the little church and set off one of the smoke alarms.

A preacher stood before the congregation and encouraged the members to attend the fall retreat at the local camp because, *"we do things with one another we don't normally do."*

2

Out of the Mouths of Kiddos

After the choir was through singing, my 3-year-old daughter stood up on the pew, threw her arms open wide like she did at home in front of the mirror and sang out loud, "LET ME GO, LOVER!" That was a little embarrassing.

One kid thought one of the angels who appeared to the shepherds at the time of the birth of Christ was named "Hark."

Another kid remarked, "We're not Christians, we're Lutherans."

I always thought those little candies called "Smarties" were the perfect thing for young children in church. They don't make a mess, they're easy to eat for even young toddlers, and they don't make a kid thirsty. Perfect, I thought, until my young daughter started to talk and was asking me to get the "Farties" out of my purse.

Our pastor was outside the church doors greeting the members of his congregation after the service. The pastors 10-year-old son was standing next to him when a car suddenly rocketed down the street in front of the church, going dangerously fast and raising gravel and dust. The pastor's son put his hands on his hips, stomped his foot and exclaimed, "What the hell does he think he's doing?"

The focus of the church school lesson was on family and that Jesus grew up in a family. Jesus' earthly father was a carpenter. I asked, "Does anyone know what a carpenter does?" All was quiet until six-year-old Alexis proudly responded, "One who lays carpet?"

When Phillip was three, his church class teacher had her first baby and named him Luke. That afternoon when Phillip's daddy came home, Phillip's mother told him to tell his daddy the new baby's name. Phillip scrunched up his face, try-

ing to remember. "Matthew?" he asked. "No," came the reply. "Mark?" "No."
Then his little face beamed and he shouted, "Romans!"

One of my work associates told me that when she and her sister were fairly
young, they went to their grandfather's funeral. The sister asked my friend if the
whole body really went to heaven. My friend said, no, just the soul. The little sister in amazement said, "You mean God just wants the feet?"

Also, my daughter at a young age was practicing for an Easter program in
which the kids were singing a song about "Hosanna, Praise Ye the Lord." Except
my young daughter thought they said something else and went around the house
singing "Lasagna, praise ye the lord."

One Sunday School kid thought Simon's last name was "Says."

My grown daughter and I were in church one Sunday morning when a family
we had never seen before sat in the pew directly in front of us. It was apparently
the children's first experience in a church. The parents entered the pew first, paying little attention to their three children who were following. When the usher
came to collect the offering, he handed the plate to the first child and all three
looked at it in amazement. They saw all the money in the plate, and each took a
handful before passing it on to the unsuspecting parents. I'll bet those kids
thought church was a great place to go! My daughter and I barely managed to
suppress our giggles.

One little kid hoped that God would throw a little party for her grandma
since she had just gone to heaven.

My husband, a preacher's son, would stick straight pins up through chair
cushions in the church foyer and hide in a nearby closer to watch the old people
sit down.

My 5-year-old daughter was saying grace before the meal and included ever so
sincerely, "And please help Jamie (her big brother) not to toot when he's in my
bedroom."

My 3-year-old son and I were sitting in Mass shortly after Easter. As the
Bishop walked down the center aisle wearing his tall, pointed hat, my son asked
loudly, "Who's the guy in the bunny ears?"

In church one Sunday, I was sitting behind a pew that held two families, each with a 3-year-old child, one a boy, and one a girl. The boy was playing quietly, and when the little girl started talking loudly, he scolded her, saying, "SHHH! We're in church. Besides, there are people sleeping here!" What makes this even more precious is that the little boy's father was the preacher!

A family with a 3-year-old girl came in late for church and sat down next to me. The little girl still had her snowsuit on and was fidgeting all over the place. She just couldn't get comfortable and would not sit still. Her mom finally unzipped the snowsuit and was peeling it off when we all noticed the reason for her irritated behavior. A coat hanger was still in the snowsuit!

My sister-in-law has two daughters, aged three years and three months. One Sunday during church, the baby was being fussy so she took her to the back of the church. The three year old noticed that Mom was gone and so was Mom's purse. She stood up on the pew, turned around, located her mother, and hollered, "MOM! Do you got my book in your purse?!"

Like the author of this book, I'm a PK, but I've decided to take the advice of a friend of mine, also a PK. She suggested we refer to ourselves as T.O.'s (Theologian's Offspring). Of course with this title comes much responsibility. My best friend would often comment in Sunday School class, "Your dad is the pastor, you should know the answers to all the questions."

In the quiet after the prayer, my newly potty-trained nephew hollered, "Mom, my big boy undies are stuck in my crackola!"

When my son was 4, he came home from Sunday School reporting that he had learned the song, "Awkward Christian Soldiers."

When my niece, Janet, and nephew, Jim, were pre-schoolers, the Sunday School class was to sing a couple of children's carols at the church's Christmas program. They practiced in their classroom and at the front of the church (minus an audience, of course) for weeks. Finally the big night arrived, and every child was scrubbed, combed, and festively clothed. The teachers herded the children to the front of the church and lined them up. The pianist began playing "Away in a manger." Jim and Janet took one look at the large congregation, and both froze.

Neither sang a note. After the program, we headed home. As we walked into the kitchen, Jim let out a giant sign. "Boy!' he declared, "it sure is a lot harder singin' than talkin'!"

I was in church with my young daughter and the congregation was "passing the peace." We shook hands with members who were sitting nearby and murmured the phrase, "Peace be with you." I had often noticed that when the entire congregation is involved, this activity creates a low, rumbling hissing sound. My daughter tugged at my sleeve and whispered, "Daddy, why does everybody say, "psss, psss, psss' when they're shaking hands.?"

My sister was sitting up front with the choir when the minister made announcements. He then asked if any others had something to announce. Imagine her embarrassed surprise when her young son called out, "I have rabbits for sale!"

As the lesson leader wrapped up a rather lengthy children's sermon, he dismissed the youngsters by saying, "Come back again to learn more about Jesus." At least half the congregation was able to observe one young boy shake his head and reply, "No way."

My son and his father were involved in the project of building a small house in the back yard for our cat. On Sunday I noticed my son had brought a tape measure along to play with in church. As I confiscated the tape measure and dropped it in my purse, my son said (loud enough for several rows of people to hear), "Don't lose that, Mom. That's the one Dad uses to build the cathouse."

Our "Joseph" in the Christmas pageant walked impressively down the aisle, leading Mary and the donkey. Suddenly, Joseph saw a man in the congregation sitting at the end of a pew and used his staff to soundly bonk this man on the head, then continued down the aisle. After the service when his horrified mother asked why on earth he had struck this gentleman, Joseph replied, *"He was making funny faces at me.*

While singing a hymn in church, my young daughter managed to change "We Exalt Thee" to "We Insult Thee."

Years ago, my young son went to the front of church to take part in the children's lesson. The topic was praising God through song and the lesson leader mentioned a few of his favorite hymns. He then asked the group of children if they had any favorite hymns. My son said, "How about the one that starts 'From the land of sky-blue waters'?" This, of course, was the jingle from a beer commercial.

My 3-year-old daughter tried to scoot herself off the pew during the sermon and the back of her bare thigh made a certain noise as it rubbed on the wooden bench. "I didn't fart, Dad," she whispered to me. I nodded and winked at her. I guess she thought I didn't believe her, so she whispered again, much louder, "I didn't fart, Dad, really." This drew chuckles from nearby worshipers. I nodded again and put my finger to my lips in a hushing motion. "Daddy, you know I didn't fart, don't you?" she wailed in full voice. I decided we'd better discuss this outside the church and scooped her up in my arms. Sobbing now, her words rang out as we walked down the aisle, "I DIDN'T FART!"

My 4-year-old daughter came home from Sunday School and told me the lesson had been all about noses. "Noses?" I asked, incredulously. "Yes, you know, little baby Noses in the basket in the river."

My daughter was gaily singing, "Jesus loves the little children, All the children of the world, Red and White and yellow stripped..."

My 4-year-old came home from Sunday School and reported that two of her little classmates stayed home sick. "So we prayed for they," she said.

My daughter wondered that since President Kennedy was Catholic if it would be okay to put a Kennedy half dollar in our Methodist collection plate.

When my three boys were small, I got into the habit of putting them down for their naps shortly before 2:00 every day so I could watch my favorite soap in peace. As my older boy reached the age where he didn't need naps any more, he was allowed to stay up and play quietly. I never thought he paid any attention to my show, which would surely be considered boring to a 5-year-old boy. But when I picked him up from Sunday School one week, his laughing teacher related that she had asked the children if anyone knew who Phillip was. My son confidently told her, "Phillip's the guy who has all the girlfriends on 'Guiding Light'."

A little boy was being disruptive during Mass. In desperation his mother gave him her Rosary to play with. Suddenly he started whirling it over his head and hollered, "Hang on, Jesus, you're goin' for a ride!"

Because of my husband's job, our family had to relocate frequently. In one city, the closest and best school in the area was a Catholic school, so that's where we enrolled our son. One day he came home and said, "OK, Mom, I want to figure this out. There are Catholics and then there are...prostitutes?"

A nurse in the surgical wing happened upon a 6-year-old boy in the recovery room. She went back out to the nurse's station and the boy's mom stepped out to grab a cup of coffee while he was still asleep. He must have rolled around a bit in his bed and inadvertently pressed the "call" button for the nurse's station. The nurse responded through the intercom, "Yes, Bobby?" There was no answer, so she tried again, "Yes, Bobby?" Still no answer. Becoming just a bit concerned, she said, "Bobby are you there?" Then came the timid reply, "Yes...God."

After my 11-year-old son came home from a children's Christmas caroling tour of area churches, he announced excitedly, "Mom, one church even gave us a standing probation."

I was sitting in church with my 11-year-old son, Willie, when the pastor asked the congregation if they had any prayer concerns. Without consulting me, Willie piped up, "Yeah. Could you have a prayer for my dog?" Keeping the smile off his face, the pastor asked with sincerity, "Of course we can, Willie. Is your dog sick?" "Oh, no, he's fine," Willie said. "But Mom said that if he doesn't stop biting the cat we're going to have to get rid of him. So, could we pray that he stops biting the cat?" We prayed. It didn't work.

My 3-year-old son would sing while sitting on the pot. He had to go #2 at church one Sunday and the whole congregation got to hear a solo.

ON the drive to church I entertained my 3-year-old nephew by teaching him to sing "Three Blind Mice." I shouldn't have because he sang it all through the church service.

Shortly after Christmas my wife, Mary, and I met another couple for dinner at a restaurant. The other couple had brought along their 2-year-old daughter. The girls mom said to her, "There's Mary. You remember Mary, don't you?" The little one's eyes grew huge as she asked, "Mary? Is this Jesus' Mom?"

When we were small, Mother used to sit in the back of the Sanctuary so that our PK antics wouldn't disturb the congregation or interrupt worship. Almost invariably, soon after we arrived at church, my little sister would stage whisper to Mom, "I have to got to the bathroom." One Sunday, upon this bathroom announcement, Mother said, "No, you don't," thinking to teach Sis to take care of her needs before arriving at church. That Sunday we were seated on some chairs at the upper end of the aisle, which was covered with a rubber runner. Suddenly Mom looked down and saw a little trickle inching its way down the slanted aisle toward the Communion Table. Never again did she question Sis's, "I hafta go…"

I overheard my young daughter recite the Lord's Prayer, "Our Father, Who Aren't in Heaven…"

A little kid was singing the Doxology: "Praise God from whom all blessings flow' Praise Him all preachers here below…"

We were in for an extra-long church service and everybody knew it. It was "Rally Sunday" on the Lutheran Church calendar. This meant extra hymns, extra Scripture readings, special music, etc. Our 70-year-old assistant pastor had to handle these duties since our regular pastor was guest preaching elsewhere. I've always wondered why a pastor can't find a way to keep the sermon SHORT on church holidays, but he seems to enjoy the captive audience, and instead really gives it his best. About 15 minutes into the sermon, my 7-year-old daughter looked up at the elderly minister and loudly whispered to me, "Doesn't his voice get tired of talking so much?"

My father-in-law's death was sudden and tragic. The funeral was emotionally draining for all who attended. My 5-year-old son was really too young to completely understand the seriousness of the occasion, which was just as well. After the final prayer at the gravesite, my son loudly asked, "Hey, can we go see where Adam and Eve are buried?" Incredibly, this was exactly what the whole group needed to ease our heavy hearts, and we all began to chuckle right there in the cemetery.

We were in church and the congregation was singing a boisterous favorite hymn, putting into it all the joy and vigor it deserved. In the silence following the grand and dramatic ending, my 5-year-old son took his hands off his ears and shouted, "Why is everyone singing so LOUD?"

My dad was the pastor in our Baptist Church, so I was used to playing in the sanctuary. The place just never held much reverence for me, since I spent so much time at the church, waiting for Dad, doing small cleaning chores, etc. My buddies loved it when I'd invite them over to the church to play. We'd have a foot race down the aisles and end it with a cannonball into the baptistry.

When I lived in northwestern Wisconsin, in red clay country, it had rained for days on end. Early one Sunday morning the pastor called to ask me to pick up a couple of girls for Sunday School. They usually rode with a couple who lived near them, but the couple was out of town that day. The girls lived off the gravel road a couple of hundred yards. My car slipped and slid all the way through the mud of the driveway, through the rain that continued to pour, up to their front door. Rather than just sound the horn, I got out of the car and sloshed to their front porch. Without opening the door, the older girl shouted to me through a window, "Go around to the back!" Her younger sister's voice was clearly heard, "Don't he know nothin'? Everybody goes to the back." So, I went back to the car, got in, and drove around to the back." I parked, got out again, and squished to the back door. This time the door was opened and the older girl told me with utter dead pan, "We ain't goin' today." After more then 13 years in the military I was able to handle it with a straight face.

As my young grandson and I were driving home from our Lutheran Church service, we passed another church which was located by a busy pedestrian crosswalk. There was a warning sign on the corner that he read slowly to me, "Watch...out...for...Presbyterians."

The primary Bible History class was reviewing the lesson on Creation. It was already established that on the sixth day God created Adam and Eve. The teacher then asked, "How did God create both Adam and Eve?" A first grader confidently and sincerely answered, "Naked!"

I have a friend whose 4-year-old daughter, Amy, would pray at night, "Now I Amy down to sleep..."

At church camp this summer, several young people were baptized. Walking back to the cabins one evening, I overheard one 7-year-old girl say that she wanted to be baptized, too. Her counselor remarked that this was wonderful, but that she was probably too young to completely understand about being baptized. The girl responded, "Oh, yes, I do! All you have to do is say 'yes, yes, yes,' to all the questions, hold your nose, and don't breathe when they put you under the water."

Our guest speaker said at the beginning of his sermon, "I'm going to preach on 'root', not 'fruit'!" His little three-year-old daughter hollered from the pew, "Oh, no! Not again!"

During a lesson on sharing, the Sunday school teacher pinched a piece of cookie off and gave it to a little kid. The next in line, a husky boy, said "I'm a lot bigger so I'll need a bigger piece."

My child came home from church and told me that they sang a song about a "crossed-eyed bear named Gladly." (Cross I bear gladly.")

A smart alec's turn to say grace: "Rub a dub, dub. Thanks for the grub. Yea God!"

While showing how a mother bird pushed the young offspring out of the nest to make them fly, the preacher made motions and said, "chirp, chirp, chirp," to emphasize the setting. A cute three-year-old took off on that, and chirped the rest of the service.

I saw a toddler taken out of church for discipline eight times, and yes, it was the pastor's kid.

"All who are prepared, come to the Lord's Table." One kid said, "Why not say, soup's on?"

In the children's Christmas play, Joseph asked the innkeeper if they had any room. The innkeeper said, "No, we have no room..." He forgot his next line but improvised by saying..."but, why don't you come in and have a drink."

While attending a funeral where the remains were cremated, they were put in an urn, wrapped, and presented to the family. My four-year-old niece turned to me and said, "Who gets to open the present?"

During church, my granddaughter was staring at my "spider looking" varicose veins on my leg and said, "Where did you get those tattoos?"

My niece's daughter Lacy, about 4 years old, sang in the Little Kids Choir. After a concert, my niece told her to "sing out" next time so we could hear her better.

At the next concert, we sat in the balcony to listen and after the first song, Lacy hollered, "Hey Mom, can you hear me up there?"

As the priest was finishing communion and wiping out the chalice, my son said, "Can we go when he gets the dishes done?"

As I returned to my seat after partaking of the communion, my four-year-old asked, "What did you get to eat this time?"

A young newcomer to a Catholic service noticed people were kneeling before they say down and asked what they were doing. The friend told her it's called a "genuflect." The youngster said, "Why don't they just call it a squat?"

Preacher doing the kid's sermon: "What has brown fur, a bushy tail, and collects nuts?" He called on one kid that said, "I know the answer is Jesus, but it sure sounds like a squirrel to me!"

The little boy's mother slipped into his bedroom while he was on his knees during prayer. She was just in time to hear, "Lord, did you see Bro. Baker walking with his eyes closed during the last prayer? He walked right into the wall when he was going to the back to greet people. Didn't you think that was funny?"

One little boy turned to his dad when the preacher got up to begin his sermon and said, "I hate this part."

Right in the middle of a church service, the nipple came off a baby's bottle, spewing milk everywhere. The parents were trying to mop up the mess with whatever was handy, but not having too much success. As the usher was passing the collection plate, another of their youngsters said loudly, "Hey, mister, my sister spilled her milk, do you have a towel?" At the end of the service, the pastor was shaking hands with the dad, and asked, "Are you the family that needed the towel?"

I was sitting in the front row with my outspoken three-year-old listening to a missionary speak on the Lord's work in Africa. The missionary apologized for his speech, which was somewhat mumbled because of a case of shingles he had on his face. My youngster asked, "Why that man talk funny?" I told him to shush, I'd tell him after church. "But, Mom, he talks so funny, how come?" On and on and on, until he said loudly, "Mom, he says ba, bla, ba, bla, ba, bla." The missionary heard this and stared at me until I shrunk. I've never been so embarrassed in my life.

It was my turn to recite the memory verse for the pastor. I said, "He that heareth me, heareth you, and un, un, un," (I couldn't remember the rest), so I said "He that heareth you, heareth me." The pastor whispered to me, "Despiseth." Oh yeah, he that despiseth me, despiseth you."

It was a Christmas service and there was a Nativity scene by the alter. The priest asked all the little children to come up to the front to see it. He asked the question, "What should be done to keep the baby Jesus warm?" One child said to put him in a blanket, another said to put straw around the manger, but the third child responded, "Shut the door!"

During the communion service, a four-year-old boy was giving his mom trouble about not letting him have any of the "cracker" that was being passed around. He said, "OK, but when the Kool-Aid man comes by, I want some!"

While standing in line receiving communion during a mass, my husband was behind me holding our 15-month-old son. He was asleep, but having outbursts of laughter like he was dreaming of something funny. I turned around to see what was going on, I thought my husband was tickling him, but decided there was nothing we could do. He would start, then stop, then start again. People were starting to get amused, and we knew things were getting out of control when the priest started to laugh. We were so embarrassed.

A normally passive little guy seemed distressed and was naughty all through the service. The parents had no idea what the problem was until after the service and the kid told them he didn't get to wear his cowboy boots to church, but daddy got to wear his!

Before the service, the elementary age kids were having a sing-along in the front of the church. One by one, a child would start singing his favorite song and the rest would join in. All went well until one boy started to sing, "When you're out of Schlitz, you're out of beer," and the others joined in.

The teacher was talking to her pre-school class about how Jesus will take your sins away. My four-year-old nephew said, "When will Jesus give them back?" She said, "He never does."

My nephew replied, "That's not very nice, take something and not give it back."

While tending one of my pre-schoolers during a sermon, my other toddler got away from me. By the time I looked back to check, he had walked down the aisle and sat on the step in front of the preacher, sucking his thumb and holding on to his blanket!

A little girl used to sit with me during services. One Sunday during the sermon, she started going through my purse, like she always did, looking for something to play with. She looked up at me and said, "I wish you had something in your purse besides dirty Kleenex's."

Caught up in the singing of, "Hide it under a bushel, No! I'm going to let it shine," one exuberant child sang, "Hide it under a bush, HELL NO! I'm going to let it shine." The teacher had a hard time taking the wind out of his sail.

One little girl couldn't understand why they would write a church song about "Bringing in the Sheets."

While preaching a sermon the pastor noticed people in the last rows looking down at the floor. He didn't think much about it until the "wave" started coming forward with each pew of people looking down. Eventually, out from under the first pew came his one-year-old, who had gotten away from his mom and crawled under all the pews on his way to the front.

We were taking turns reading from the Old Testament in our Bible class. It was one boy's turn to read about the priests in the synagogue. This word was new to him but he did his best by sounding it out, "sin-a-go-gue."

My five-year-old daughter kept telling us about Adam and Steve in her Sunday school class. It took a while before we figured out that she meant Adam and Eve.

A young mother was tugging her newly-potty-trained daughter down the aisle. The mother wasn't paying much attention because the reason her daughter wouldn't come gently is because her panties were down by her ankles. She didn't like them and by golly, she wasn't going to wear them!

In the middle of a church service, a little girl about 4 took off running through the pews. The dad got up and ran after her and suddenly it became a game of chase me and catch me. As soon as she was almost caught, she would duck under a couple of pews and escape. She out-maneuvered her dad until the preacher asked for help.

I used to enjoy sitting behind a certain little boy to see how many people he hit with his Cheerios.

It was Easter Sunday Mass and during the service the priest was walking down the aisle throwing holy water over the congregation. My three-year-old got hit and said, "Hey, who spit on me?"

As an usher passing the collection plate one Sunday, I waited while a couple who had given their daughter a dime struggled to get her to let go of it. As they pried it from her fingers, she angrily yelled, "I don't see why I have to pay anything, I didn't want to come here anyway!"

We drove by the Grace Lutheran Church the other day and my five-year-old daughter said, "Grace who?"

Years ago, my three-year-old cousin was standing on the pew beside me holding his own hymnal when he leaned over and asked, "What channel are we on?"

I was in a health food store when a fellow with long hair, beard, and white robe came in to do some shopping. I could feel my toddler staring at this man, but felt there was nothing I could do about it. All of a sudden the ice broke when my seven-year-old said to her, "No, Regan, it's not God!"

A minister was trying to explain the Lord's Supper to a group of children. He compared it to having a kind of party. He asked the group, "What do people do at your house when there's a party? Hoping for an answer of "celebrate" or "praise," one kid said, "Go crazy!"

When the bread was being passed during communion, I heard a little child yell, "I want some cake!"

As we were passing the First Christian Church, My kindergartner said, "That's really neat." I asked her what she meant, and she answered, "The first one." I was still confused and asked again what she meant. She said, "Is that church really the first one?"

When my boys were little, if one of our goldfish died, we would have a little funeral, say the Lord's Prayer, and flush the fish down the toilet. As my boys grew up and had their own families, they carried on the same tradition.

While attending the funeral of my granddaughter's other grandmother, while barely old enough to talk, she said, you guessed it, "Are we gonna flush her?"

My family always sat in the back of the church during mass. One Sunday my husband had to usher. When the time came for him to go to the altar, he stood up and began his long walk to the front. I took my eye off my three-year-old for one second, and by the time I looked back, he had taken off running after his daddy. I caught up to him right as my husband stopped at the altar.

After getting my offering envelope out of my purse, my little son said, "Mommy, Mommy!" I told him to hush because grandpa was about to preach. He kept on and on, until in desperation, I asked him what was the matter. He whispered loudly, "You snapped your purse shut on my finger!" Sure enough, I had.

Our pastor was doing his children's sermon by radio broadcast, and the topic was "Rules." When he asked the children if they had any rules at their houses, one four-year-old piped up and blurted over the P.A. system, "We can't pee in the yard!"

When my son was about six, he and I discussed the resurrection and the meaning of Easter. I explained things the best I could to a lad of his understanding, and he said, "Now I've heard everything."

A new kid joined the second grade at a Catholic school. On the second day, he raised his hand and signed #1. Sister Christine says, "Mark, you may leave the room." Mark left but was soon back saying, "I can't find it, Sister!"

Sister Christine asked Bernard to go with Mark and help him find it. He and Mark left the room and in five minutes returned and took their seats. Mark was grinning from ear to ear, "We found it Sister, I had my pants on backwards!"

I was behind the stage curtain of our Fellowship Hall. I was aware of several kids on the stage steps, but they didn't know I could hear their conversation. One boy, about five, told another of the same age, "Randy thinks you're a nerd!" That phrase caught my attention, and I assumed I would be in the midst of breaking up a quarrel within minutes. However, the statement that followed caused a deafening silence: "What kind of nerd?"

If we each could but measure our responses with such wisdom!

As a young boy was being dragged out of the service for discipline, he hollered, "Somebody have mercy!"

I heard about a very strict Mennonite pastor who took his five-year-old son out of church for discipline. The boy thought he was being treated unfairly. Later that day, the pastor took his son to a men's business meeting and made him sit in the corner until the meeting was over.

At this time the boy got his revenge. He said to the group, "My dad will probably deny this, but he smokes sometimes!"

During a solemn ceremony, as the altar boys lit candles, our three-year-old sang out, "Happy Birthday to you!"

While keeping busy during the sermon, a little boy's toy car rolled away from him, going several pews ahead. Before his mother realized, he had crawled under the pews, through several people's legs and retrieved the car. From five pews ahead, he stood up and hollered, "Mom, I found it!"

A kid pointed to the preacher's head and said, "You got an empty spot up there." What he meant was a "bald spot."

While teaching a children's class, the teacher asked the question, "Who wrote the book of Psalms?" One perky said "Psalmbody."

On Lutheran Confirmation day, the pastor asked the question, "Who started the church?" One excited boy eagerly waved his hand, much to his mothers pride, and when called on said, "Martin Luther King!" The pastor stopped, the mother melted.

"There were 12 loaves in 2 dishes."

The kids were playing church and one said, "Jesus, if you don't behave, I'll have Joseph get the ruler!"

A kid says, "If we were made out of the dust of the earth, why don't we turn to mud when we get rained on?"

While riding quietly in the hearse on the way to bury my husband, my six-year-old grandson said to the driver, "Man, you got a great set of wheels!"

As I watched a mom force her little son to put his quarter in the collection plate, the boy said, "Mommy, that's mine!"

I was in a service when a little boy (the pastor's kid) stood on the pew and hollered, "That's enough, Dad!"

My four-year-old daughter was sure she could handle going to the bathroom all by herself. About the middle of the communion service, I started wondering if she was taking care of business or not, when I heard a yell from the bathroom, "Mom, I'm done!"

During a "Pew Packers" session, where the small children answer Bible questions, the teacher asked a little boy named Seth who the first three sons of Adam and Eve were. He could only think of Cain and Abel until the teacher said, "The third one has your name. The boy said, "Cain, Abel, and Seth!"

When the teacher asked the little girl next to him to recite them, she said, "Cain, Abel, and Janie!"

A pre-school member of my Sunday school class was not very impressed with the story of Martha anointing Jesus' feet with perfume. He exclaimed, "We put perfume here (pointing to his armpit), not on our feet!" On the way home from Sunday school his father asked him what he had learned that day. He responded that the story had been about some women putting deodorant on Jesus. His father had some questions for me the next Sunday.

After Dad got back from partaking of the Communion wine, my little sister hollered, "Mom, Dad smells like he's been to the club again!"

Every time this elderly man would lead us in prayer, it seemed his pleas would get longer and longer. One Sunday as he prayed, my three-year-old niece got impatient and hollered loudly, "AMEN!"

The whole congregation started laughing and the man concluded his prayer quickly.

A friend of mine tells of a little girl who attended church with her mother and suddenly began to feel ill.

"Mama," she said, "I have to go throw up."

"Hurry around to the little garden in back of the church," said the parent.

Presently the girl was back and her mother asked, "Were you there and back already?"

"Oh, I didn't have to go way out there," replied the tot. "I saw a box in the back of the church which said, 'For the sick'."

I could tell my three-year-old son was scared as I took him to the doctor to get a bad splinter removed. I told him that it was going to be OK because Jesus was going to be there with him.

As we sat down in the full reception room, he looked up at me and whispered, "Which one's Jesus?"

"Job, Psalms, Proverbs,...Enthusiastics."

One's kid's definition of Lent: "It's the stuff that gets stuck in the dryer thing."

While teaching my preschool class about guilt and what it means to do bad things, I asked one child if she felt bad after she disobeyed her mommy. She answered, "No, but it makes my mommy feel bad."

As I showed my 1st grade class a picture of Jesus holding up his hands and preaching to his disciples, I asked them what they thought he was saying. One child said, "He's telling them to be good." Another said, "To not be naughty." The third child had a different approach. She said, "He's telling them that he'll be back next Sunday."

As a man with a husky voice read the scriptures from the back of the church instead of the customary front pulpit, my three-year-old said, "Is that God?"

I was teaching a kindergarten class a lesson about Jesus dying on the cross, and I asked "Who knows what Jesus said before he died?"

No one said anything for the longest time until one fellow raised his hand and said, "Jesus said, 'Good Luck, everybody'."

After watching a teenager being baptized, my youngest said, "How old do you have to be to be advertised?"

"Be what?" I asked.

He answered, "You know, advertised…like when they put you under the water."

This little boy always sang, "Jesus loves me, this I know. For the milo tells me so." He lived on a farm.

Every kid in class was supposed to use the word "heaven" in a sentence.
The first kid said, "When I die I hope to go to heaven."
The second kid said, "Heaven is where God lives."
The third kid said, "My mom is heaven another headache."

One young fellow almost got them all correct. "Psalms, Proverbs, Ecclesiastics, Song of Salmon."

My three-year-old son and I were looking at the jet streams in the sky and he asked, "Daddy can we go to heaven on one of those planes?"

My six-year-old daughter was asked what church she attended. She thought and said, "I can't remember exactly, but it's one of the Lutheran churches." Later she exclaimed, "I remember now. It's the German Shepherd Lutheran Church!"

We took our five-year-old nephew to church for the first time. When communion was being observed, one of the ushers started giving the prayer for the bread. My nephew asked, "What's he doing?" I answered, "We're having the Lord's Supper."
"Oh, good," he said, "I'm hungry."

One kid was happy that she belonged to her church, "cause you don't have to go through a percolator to get to heaven like the Catholics do."

A five-year-old's explanation of Creation: "...then God put Adam to sleep and took out a wishbone to make the lady."

I told my son, "No, on Super Bowl Sunday, when the pastor raises his hands to praise God, it doesn't mean 'Touchdown'!"

A friend asked my five-year-old what part of church he liked best. He said, "The going home part."

It was a habit for our family to recite scriptures on the way to church each Sunday morning. When it came time for my youngest daughter to repeat the selected scripture after all the other kids, instead of repeating "Keep your tongue from lies and deceit," she said "Keep your tongue from lice and disease."

As I was sitting through a rather lengthy sermon, my daughter's little neighborhood friend who was sitting with us hollered, "I HATE CHURCH AND SO DOES MY DAAAAAAD!"
I thought I was going to die!

My daughter was talking to my five-year-old grandson about the meaning of Lent. She asked him what he would like to give up during this period and he thought and thought and finally said, "I think I'll give up Sunday School."
She remarked that that isn't what she meant. He thought again and said, "OK, I'll give up church then."

As a beautiful white dove flew overhead, my four-year-old daughter asked, "Is that the 'Holy Dove'?"

As the chimes rang in our church, my three-year-old son said quietly, "It sounds like Taco Bell."

My daughter likes to brag about her pastor daddy going to school at a "cemetery."

Our four-year-old daughter remarked how much she liked "Pom Pom" Sunday.

Noticing a lot of special decorations at our Easter Service, my daughter remarked about how this reminded her of her birthday party.

One kid thought the special name given to the first Wednesday in Lent was "Leap Year."

This kid almost had it right when he said, "I believe in Jesus Christ, the only forgotten Son of God."

I asked my grandson if he would like to go to the altar with me. He said, "No, but would you bring me back something to eat?"

While we were waiting in the Communion line, my niece asked, "Isn't there any express lane?"

As is taught, when we are baptized we become "new creatures in Christ." One youngster said, "Baptism makes us new animals for God."

One little fellow was overheard as singing: "Microwave the board ashore, alleluia."

At this Lutheran church, the question was asked in the 1st grade class, "Can anyone name the four Gospels?"
One boy answered, "Matthew, Mark, Luther, and John."

I asked my class why Jesus could do miracles. One boy said, "Because he knew magic."

I showed my class a picture of Jesus and one of them asked why he wasn't smiling. A less than enthusiastic child remarked, "Because he had to go to church again."

As we parked our car in the church parking lot, I saw the new vicar going into the church. I asked my six-year-old daughter if she knew who that man was. She answered, "Yes, that's the man that wants to be a pastor when he grows up."

The pastor's first sentence of his sermon was "Lo, I am with you always." My restless daughter said, "Oh, no. We're going to be here a long time!"

The children's sermon was about "Grudges." The pastor asked the class what a grudge was.
One boy raised his hand and said, "It's where you put the car."

The question was asked a kindergarten class "Who was Jesus?" One kid said, "He invented the Bible book."

As my son looked up at the statue of Jesus on the cross, he remarked, "Holy cow, Mom. There's God!"

As we walked into mass, my daughter looked up at the cross and asked, "Does that T stand for our name?" (Tonniges)

The young boy was reciting the books of the Old Testament: "Amos, Obadiah,..." He couldn't remember any more so the teacher gave him this hint, "He was swallowed by a whale," she remarked.
The boy sparked, "Oh yeah! Pinocchio!"

I have a friend whose young son took a straw out of her purse while she wasn't looking. As she listened to the sermon, he held it loosely in the palm of one hand, and by smacking one end with the other hand, launched it into the lap of an unsuspecting worshipper, three rows ahead.

One kid said Mary's husband was named Virg. "Yes," he said, "Virg 'n Mary!"

One Sunday my three-year-old daughter was sitting on my lap. She was just learning how to zip, snap, button, etc., and she was fiddling with the buttons on my blouse during the sermon. Of course, I was keeping half an eye on her, but I soon realized that she wasn't having any success, so I devoted my attention to the sermon.

After the lesson, the congregation rose and I stood and shifted my daughter to one hip. We were only a few rows from the front of the church, so Pastor had a clear view of us from the stage. He was trying to be discreet, but I could tell he was sending me an urgent message with his eyes pointedly staring at me! I felt a little uncomfortable, wondering what it could be, until I finally realized my little girl had learned how to button (or should I say UN-button) and my entire blouse was gaping open.

My young son was watching the people in our congregation go up to the front for communion. He asked me why they were doing this and what does communion mean. I explained to him that this was a very special way of remembering that Jesus had suffered for us all by being nailed to the cross and dying for our sins. This made him look very sober, and then he asked earnestly, "Well, where were the policemen?"

My twelve-year-old daughter and I always pray together before she goes to bed. On one recent evening I left her room grinning. As part of her petitions she had prayed, "And help Daddy get a raise soon—that's 'soon' in people time, God, not in your time."

A young pastor was driving home from church with his four-year-old son. The boy noticed a man walking his beautiful Dalmation dog and said with excitement, "Look, Dad! A damnation!"

It was Christmas Eve in rural upstate New York. The children were prepared to reenact the Nativity scene one more time. The littlest ones had been included as well, with short, simple lines such as "angels singing," "crowds rejoicing," etc. Nathan's turn came. Dorothy stood in front of the children ready to prompt them when trouble came. Nathan mumbled something. Dorothy shook her head and stage-whispered lines to him. He mumbled again. She repeated the words. With a frown, Nathan drew a deep breath and shouted, "Bells are ringing, I TOLD YOU!!!"

In a small-town church in western Kentucky, I was giving my usual children's message. It was around Christmas time and we were discussing the colors that often symbolize the holiday. Trying to bring the point home to them, I asked, "When you ride through town, what do you see that's red and green?" After pondering awhile and coming up with everything but the correct response, one child piped up, "Tractors!"

The church of my childhood has a very large and formal Georgian-style sanctuary, with a long, narrow chancel area. At the very back of the chancel was a white altar. When I was a little kid I never saw anyone go up to the altar except the pastors, so I imagined it was a sort of Protestant Holy of Holies, a place where God dwelt, or maintained a vacation home when things got too hectic in heaven. At the very least, I thought that the altar housed objects too sacred ever to be seen, something like saintly relics in medieval cathedrals.

Twenty or so years later I happened to be helping out with something at church one weekday and wandered into the sanctuary. Imagine my shock when I saw the grizzled old sexton calmly walk up to the altar, unlock the front panel, open it and take out a mop and bucket. My Holy of Holies was actually a broom closet.

My six-year old daughter was writing the Lord's Prayer for a Sunday School project. She asked me how to spell "rotten." Why would you need to spell that?" I asked. "You know," she answered, "Our Father, who rotten heaven."

When we caught our 7-year-old son in a lie, we told him that we might not always find out but God will always know. He said, "Yeah, but He won't tell you."

While driving home from church my 4-year-old daughter asked why the pastor was talking about God's rat (wrath). At least she was trying.

My 4-year-old son was tickled that I was getting re-married because I told him his new daddy and I would probably have a little brother or sister for him to play with some day. Immediately after the "I do's" he said loudly, "Mom, now you can have that baby!" (I wasn't pregnant.)

At the end of his sermon, the visiting pastor introduced his family to the congregation. His wife, his oldest son and his daughter stood as he called their names. Their 5-year-old son was nowhere to be seen. No one had seen him leave the service and people were starting to get concerned…until they found him sound asleep under the pew where the family was sitting.

I took my 3-year-old daughter out of church to go to the bathroom. As she was washing her hands, an elderly lady came into the bathroom. My daughter looked up and asked her, "Are you tired of church, too?"

The preacher lifted up his Bible and read from the Book of Revelation. My daughter whispered to me, "Good, he's almost done with the Bible."

My 13-year-old son, Joseph, had a big red "N" painted on his cheek for the Nebraska football game on Saturday night. The following morning he was supposed to be the altar boy at first mass. His mom and I were going to take an early walk and go to second mass that morning, so before we left the house we made sure he was awake and gave him instructions to take a shower before he went to church. After the second mass, the Priest approached us and mentioned that our son must be a big football fan. He hadn't taken a shower or washed the "N" off his face.

One 5th-grader's sermon summary: "The sermon was about the 6th Commandment, which is adultery and the pastor's trip to California.

While driving past the cemetery, one little girl said she wanted to see someone rise from the dead.

A wailing ambulance could be heard from blocks away. The Mom said to her little girl, "Let's say a prayer." The girl followed with, "Dear God, please let me have a Barbie doll for my birthday."

One kid asked what God's last name was.

Asked what the Wise Men brought baby Jesus, one little guy said, "Gold, 50 cents and myrrh."

One day the minister of my Protestant church called on the phone. My 5-year-old daughter answered and hollered to me, "Mom, it's for you. It's the priest!"

One summer evening I told my 6-year-old son to go inside and take a bath. He replied, "Why, Mom? God hasn't even turned off the lights yet."

Last Christmas my sister sent my 4-year-old son a Mother Mary medallion. He asked who she was and I told him that Mary was the mother of Jesus. He looked serious and asked, "Did she have a little lamb?"

My daughter has a little Jewish friend who told her they don't have Merry Christmas, but Happy Hanukkah. My daughter replied, "We have a harmonica, too."

During the church play, my 5-year-old son forgot his line. Without being too obvious, I whispered it to him, "I am the light of the world." He beamed and proudly said, "My Mom is the light of the world!"

My 5-year-old son had a Catholic friend spending the weekend with us. On Sunday morning we were going to church and Sunday School at our church and I thought I should call the friend's mom and make sure it was OK that he went with us to our church. I told the boys what I was going to do and the friend said, "I'm not Catholic, I'm ambidextrous."

Sitting in Sunday School I knew I was in trouble because I had forgotten to memorize a Bible verse. I was searching my memory, trying to come up with a verse—any verse would do. Right as the teacher called on me, something popped into my head. "In God we trust," I confidently recited. "Nice try," replied the teacher.

In the middle of a sermon I leaned over and whispered something to my 3-year-old daughter. I guess my breath wasn't too good because she leaned back and said, "Phew, Dad, did you toot?" I didn't think it was very funny, but the people in front of us sure did.

Each of our children gives money from their piggy banks, which we send to support orphaned children in Africa. My very generous 4-year-old said, "Mommy, I like it when I give all my money to the children in my piggy bank."

As the wise men walked onto the stage at the Christmas play, one 3-year-old boy hollered, "INJUNS!!"

At a Methodist Vacation Bible School, the first grade teacher asked her class, "What did Paul convert all the people to?" One boy raised his hand and answered, "Lutherans?"

I grew up in a pastor's home where there was lots of praying. One day in Junior High School I was asked to lead the Pledge of Allegiance. At the end…"with liberty and justice for all," I inadvertently added, "In Jesus' name, Amen."

In a group of young children, we were having a chain prayer. A sweet little red-headed boy was the last one to pray. He simply said, "In Jesus' name, Amen." I said, "Jimmy, can't you think of anything to pray for?" To which he replied, "It's already done been prayed for."

As my husband was preaching one of his favorite sermons at a new church, my 7-year-old son whispered to me, "I've heard this one before."

A young preacher ended his sermon with the reminder that the church was there to help anyone who needed assistance. He invited members to come forward during the next hymn and ask for the church's prayers and help. When the hymn began, the preacher's three-year-old son scampered out of his pew and sat down at his fathers' feet. When the hymn ended and no one else had come forward, the preacher sat down by his young son and asked, "What are you doing up here?" The boy replied, "I need help, Daddy, my shoe is untied."

We bought a puppy and named him Michelob, pronounced just like the beer brand. A few weeks later our 4-year-old son went to the front of the church for the children's sermon. When the pastor asked the kids to name some things they were thankful for, our son's hand shot up and he exclaimed, "I'm thankful for Michelob!"

One little boy thought the vows the bride and groom were going to say were A,E,I,O,U."

My 7-year-old daughter was fidgeting during the sermon. I told her to sit still and stop whining. She replied, "Well, if I can't whine, what am I supposed to do?"

I asked the 3-year-olds in my Sunday School class if they remembered the story about the two little boys who lived in a tent on the sand. Little Christy jumped up and shouted, "I know! Jacob and See Saw!"

In my 3-year-old daughter's Sunday School class, the children were encouraged to memorize portions of Bible verses. On Sunday, Sara's verse was, "Peace. Be still." On the way to church she said, "Mommy, I know my Bible verse—'Please be still.'"

A friend of mine was taking her young son to confession. When she told him where they were going, for some reason he seemed overjoyed and very excited. Whey they got to church and walked inside she found out the reason. He thought she'd said they were goin' fishin'.

A certain lady's children were always naughty in church and one Sunday as they rose for the benediction she grabbed one of them and whispered loudly, "Why are you kids so bad in church?" The child thought a moment, then answered, "Because, Mom, we get tired at looking at big butts."

While in church singing HOW GREAT THOU ART, my 5-year-old son tugged at my shirt and asked, "Who's Art?"

The preacher was giving a children's sermon and one of the questions he asked the kids was, "Who was the oldest man who ever lived?" The anticipated answer was "Methuselah." One kid raised his hand and answered, "Jesus!" I guess the answer "Jesus" works more times than not, so it was a good guess.

When I was a kid my mom would threaten me with, "The Devil's going to get you," when I was naughty. One day, after behaving worse than usual, she hollered, "The Devil's coming to get you right now!" A second later there was a loud knock at the front door, which scared the heebie jeebie's out of me.

It was Easter and I was teaching my 3rd grade Sunday School class about Jesus on the cross. I presented this talk very seriously and took a great deal of time explaining things. Right as I finished, one little boy raised his hand and said, "My puppies have worms."

Our pastor walked past us in church and my 3-year-old son said, "Hi, God!"

A mother was teaching her 3-year-old daughter the Lord's Prayer. For several evenings at bedtime, she repeated it after her mother. One night she said she was ready to solo. The mother listened with pride as the girl carefully enunciated each word right up to the end. "And lead us not into temptation," she prayed, "but deliver us some e-mail. Amen."

A mother was preparing pancakes for her sons Kevin, 5, and Ryan, 3. The boys began to argue over who would get the first pancake. Their mother saw the opportunity for a moral lesson. "If Jesus were here, He would say, 'Let my brother have the first pancake. I can wait.'" Kevin turned to his younger brother and said, "Ryan, you be Jesus."

A little girl became restless as the preacher's sermon dragged on and on. Finally she whispered to her mother, "Mommy, if we give him the money now, will he let us go?"

A Sunday School teacher asked a little boy, "Bobby, do you believe in the devil?" "No," the boy said, "he's just like Santa Claus. I think it's my dad."

One little boy prayed, "Dear God, We had a good time at church today. Wish you could have been there."

A little boy began his prayer, "Dear Harold." His father interrupted and asked, "How come you called God 'Harold'?" The boy replied, "That's what they call him in church. You know, 'Our Father, who art in Heaven, Harold be Thy name."

A 6-year-old boy was overheard reciting the Lord's prayer, "And forgive us our trash passes as we forgive those who passed trash against us."

One family of children grew up singing the line from Silent Night as follows: "Ground round virgin, Mother and child."

During the minister's prayer, there was a loud whistle from one of the back pews. Gary's mother was horrified. She silenced him quickly and after church asked, "Gary, whatever made you do such a thing?" Gary answered soberly, "I've been praying that God would teach me to whistle...and He just then did!"

My 4-year-old daughter was drawing in church when she dropped her papers. She put her pencil crossways in her mouth as she reorganized. Then she looked up at me and said (with the pencil still in her mouth), "Mom, I can't find my pencil anywhere!"

My 3-year-old daughter was in love with her animated Cinderella movie. At the end of the hymn "Reach for Thy Coming," she inadvertently added, "Bibbity, Bobbity, Boo."

When our kids were little, my husband did a lot of substitute preaching for churches in the area. One Sunday our young family arrived at a new church and discovered the entire basement was flooded. My 4-year-old son said, "Hey, I like this church! It has a swimming pool."

One Sunday School teacher asked the class to name some of the apostles. One kid said, "Peter, Paul and...Mary?"

One 16-year-old preacher's kid thought he was pretty cool after he snuck out in the middle of a church service. As he drove quietly out of the parking lot he turned on his CB radio and squawked over it to a friend, "Hey, I just skipped out of church and my dad doesn't know it! He found out later that the church PA system picked it up loud and clear.

Six-year-old Angie and her 4-year-old brother Joel were sitting together in church. Joel giggled, sang and talked out loud. Finally his big sister had had enough. "You're not supposed to talk out loud in church." "Why? Who's going to stop me?" Joel asked. Angie pointed to the back of the church and said, "See those two men standing by the door? They're the hushers."

In the middle of a sermon, a mom whispered to her 4-year-old son to "talk less and listen more." He replied, "But, Mom, my mouth wants to say things."

My grandson was visiting one day when he asked, "Grandma, do you know how you and God are alike?" I mentally polished my halo while I asked, "No, how are we alike?" "You're both old," he replied.

A Sunday School class was studying the Ten Commandments. They were ready to discuss the last one. The teacher asked if anyone could tell her what the 10th Commandment was. Susie raised her hand, stood tall and quoted, "Thou shall not take the covers off the neighbor's wife."

During the holiday season my family and I were driving down the street. My 3-year-old daughter hollered, "Jeeeesus!" It sounded like she was swearing so I told her not to speak about Jesus that way. Her older brother then informed me that she was referring to Jesus in the Nativity scene we had just driven by.

The pastor said something about the Dead Sea Scrolls and my 5-year-old son whispered to me, "Hey, I've seen a dead squirrel too."

One little girl told her Sunday school teacher that Jesus' mother was named "Mary Christ."

A 10-year-old, under the tutelage of her grandmother, was becoming quite knowledgeable about the Bible. Then one day she astonished Grandma by asking, "Which virgin was the mother of Jesus? The Virgin Mary, or the King James virgin?"

A little boy was overheard praying, "Lord, if you can't make me a better boy, don't worry about it. I'm having a really good time just the way I am!"

My son and his wife were heavily involved in a bus ministry for several years. The children were allowed to choose their favorite songs to sing while on the way to church in the bus. One little boy was very unhappy and complained to my son because no one would sing his favorite song. My son assured him that of course they would sing his favorite son and asked him what it was. The boy answered, "Take this Job and Shove it."

After my 4-year-old daughter concluded her prayer with "Amen," she looked at me and asked, "Why can't I say, 'A-woman?'"

Right after I became a Christian and turned my life around, I was roped into teaching my daughter's preschool Bible class. I wasn't sure how she would react having her dad in charge—and, to be truthful, I wasn't quite sure what I was getting into. The class was discussing what they did to help their moms and dads. My daughter kept waving her hand and I finally (and reluctantly had to call on her. She said, "I help my daddy when he's watching a ball game." As much as I didn't want to, I had to ask her to explain, She said, "I help you not to say—and—!" She ripped them off just like I used to.

The question for the confirmand was, "Jesus spoke with a _____ at a well about living water." The correct response was "Samaritan woman." The unexpected answer from one confirmand was "Southern accent."

I remember when the preacher's kids took their dad's sermon notes out of his Bible one Sunday morning and replaced them with comic book pages. As I recall, the church floors were sure polished for a long time after that incident.

My three-year-old daughter was being very naughty during church, worse than usual, and to keep her still during the upcoming prayer, I decided to pin her between my knees, In the quiet before the prayer, she folded her hands and prayed out loud, "Dear Lord, you gotta help me, I'm trapped!"

Right after a prayer, my baby brother burped so loud I thought the windows were going to break.

I was teaching my son's kindergarten Sunday school class and asked who the first man and woman were. One kid said, "Adam and Eve." My son responded, "No, it's Mary and John"—meaning Joseph. Not only did my own kid give the wrong answer, but his wrong answer was wrong.

In his sermon, my pastor mentioned something about winter coming on and how we had all better be getting our sheep gates in order. My six-year-old daughter said, "Sheet cake?" At least she was listening...sort of.

My daughter's family used to attend a church where everything was quite informal. The pastor wore a suit rather than a robe, and the congregation dressed casually. Then the family moved to a different city and joined a church where things were more formal. The women of the congregation wore dresses, the men wore suits and ties, and the pastor wore a fancy robe with formal accessories. The first time my five-year-old grandson saw the pastor, he exclaimed, "Why is that man wearing his bathrobe?"

My wife was giving our newborn his bath, and my daughter was watching. Suddenly she came running to me and hollered, "Dad, BJ's biblical cord fell off!"

As we were passing through a small town, my daughter said, "That's weird. That sign says it's a Baptist Catholic church. I've never heard of such a thing." We turned the car around for another look. The sign said, "St. John the Baptist Catholic Church."

One little girl always started her prayers with, "God bless me, God bless Mommy and Daddy..." and so on. She remarked to her mom, "Do you know why I say God bless me first? Because I like me best."

Kids responses to Bible questions:

WHAT ARE PASTORS?

> He works for God.
> He wrote the Bible.
> Pastor's tell you about Jesus and smile.
> They marry people that need it.
> He's the bald guy that sings real loud.
> They give money to poor people.
> We always have to shake his hand after church.
> He's the person that does most of the talking at church.
> Pastor's make my mom happy and my dad mad.
> Pastors eat a lot at picnics.
> They talk a long time about stuff.
> They go to church all the time.
> He gets all the money in the plates.
> He's the one in the robe that looks like Jesus.
> Pastors read the Bible a lot.
> Do you mean the preacher? He's the guy that works at the church with the janitor.

Samson played the Philistines with the ax of the apostles.

Unleavened bread is bread made with no ingredients.

Moses went to the top of Mount Cyanide to get the Ten Commandments.

The seventh commandment? Thou shalt not admit adultery.

Joshua led the Hebrews In the Battle of Geritol.

Solomon had 300 wives and 700 porcupines.

Jesus was born because Mary had an immaculate contraption.

The people who followed Jesus were called the 12 decibels.

The first book of the Bible is called Guinessis.

One of the opossums was St. Matthew.

Adam and Eve were created from an apple.

Paul preached acrimony, which is another name for marriage.

David fought the Finkelsteins, a race of people who lived in biblical times.

The Jews had trouble throughout their history with unsympathetic Genitals.

"The message came to Abraham that he should bear a son, and Sarah, who was listening behind the door, laughed."

"Job had one trouble after another. He lost all his cattle and all his children and then he had to go and live alone with his wife in the desert."

"John the Baptist was beheaded for dancing too persistently with the daughter of Herodotus."

In what order do the Gospels come? "One after another."

"The Great Flood was sent because of the large number of dirty people."

From a Catechism question: "…to love, honor and suckle my Father and Mother."

If any man smite thee on the right cheek, you should…"Smite him on the other also."

"The greatest miracle in the Bible is when Joshua told his son to stand still and he obeyed him."

Who was sorry when the Prodigal son returned? "The fatted calf."

"John the Baptist was a centaur which means that he was half man and half horse. It says his head was on a charger."

"Lazarus used to eat the food out of the rich man's stable."

"The Tower of Babel was the place where Solomon kept his wives."

"The Mosiac Law was a law compelling people to have their floors laid with colored stones."

"Jacob was a patriarch who brought up his twelve sons to be patriarchs, but they did not take to it."

"Jacob didn't eat much, as a rule, except when there was a famine in the land."

"Esau was a man who wrote fables and sold his copyright for a mess of potash."

"Abraham, after the sacrifice of Issac, called the place Rio Janeiro."

"The Bible is against bigamy when it says that no man can serve two masters."

"Gomorrah was Sodom's wife and Lot had to flee with them."

"David slew Goliath with a catapult."

"If David had one fault it was a slight tendency to adultery."

"Little is known about the prophet Elijah, except that he once went for a cruise with a widow."

"Sarah was Abraham's half-wife, otherwise mid-wife, sometimes called columbine."

"The synagogues were rich Jews who didn't like to work, and believed in Christ."

"Before a man could become a monk he had to have his tonsils cut."

"Christianity was introduced into Britain by the Romans."

"Those who did not accept the Orthodox faith were hereditary."

"In the days of Joseph the Egyptians gave refuse to the Israelites."

"Buddha is worshipped chiefly in Budda Pest."

"The gods of the Indians are chiefly Mohammed and Buddah and in their spare time they do a lot of carving."

A boy was watching his father, a pastor, write a sermon. "How do you know what to say?" he asked. "Why, God tells me." "Oh, then why do you keep crossing things out?"

One summer evening, during a violent thunderstorm, a mother was tucking her small boy into bed. She was about to turn off the light, when he asked, with a tremor in his voice, "Mommy, will you sleep with me tonight?" The mother smiled and gave him a reassuring hug. "I can't, dear," she said. "I have to sleep with your Daddy." A long silence was broken, at last, by his shaky little voice: "The big sissy."

Nine-year-old Joey was asked by his mother what he had learned in Sunday School. "Well, Mom, our teacher told how God sent Moses behind enemy lines on a rescue mission to lead the Israelites out of Egypt. When he got to the Red Sea, he had his engineers build a pontoon bridge, and all the people walked across safely. He used his walkie-talkie to radio headquarters and call in an air strike. They sent in bombers to blow up the bridge and all the Israelites were saved. "Now, Joey, is that REALLY what your teacher taught you?" his mother asked. "Well, no, Mom, but if I told it the way the teacher did, you'd never believe it!"

Finding one of her students making faces at others on the playground, Ms. Smith stopped to gently reprove the child. Smiling sweetly, the Sunday School teacher said, "Bobby, when I was a child, I was told that if I made ugly faces, it would freeze and I would stay like that." Bobby looked up into her face and replied, "Well, Ms. Smith, you can't say you weren't warned!"

A little boy was attending his first wedding. After the service, his cousin asked him, "How many women can a man marry?" "Sixteen," the boy responded. His cousin was amazed that he knew the answer so quickly. "How do you know that?" "Easy," the little boy said. "All you have to do is add it up, like the Bishop said: 4 better, 4 worse, 4 richer, 4 poorer."

3

Out of the Mouths of Typewriters

This afternoon there will be meetings in the south and north ends of the church. Children will be baptized at both ends.

Tuesday at 4 p.m. there will be an ice cream social. All ladies giving milk, please come early.

This being Easter Sunday, we will ask Mrs. Johnson to come forward and lay an egg on the alter.

The services will close with "Little Drops of Water." One of the ladies will start quietly, and the rest of the congregation will join in.

The ladies of the church have cast off clothing of every kind and they may be seen in the church basement on Friday afternoon.

A bean supper will be held Saturday evening in the basement. Music will follow.

The rosebud on the altar is to announce the birth of David Alan Belser, the sin of Rev. and Mrs. Julius Belser.

We will be distributing VBS flies this afternoon.

The ladies are invited to a miscellaneous bridle tea.

As she was preparing to come to church last Sunday, she suffered a small stoke.

Thank you for your sympathy and the lovely pot plant.

The topic for the Elder's Bible class will be "Sinplicity of Christianity."

Next Friday we will be serving hot gods for lunch.

As soon as there weather clears, the men will have a goof outing.

Adult dinner menu: Road beef, potatoes, and gravy.

Half of our difficulty in doing anything worthy of high calling is the shrinking anticipation of its possible after consequences.

Join us in the fellowship room for impromptu adult entertainment.
The nursery is back to the right. The switch is on the wall.

To meet again in that home, where there will be no sorrow, no death, and no rears.

In the classifieds of a church magazine, an ad was inserted about a church looking for a new minister. It said, "Starts August 6, 1991. Send resume by June 1. Include wife, transcripts, and references."

Don't forget, Saturday the ladies in the Secret Sister program will be revealing themselves.

Sermon outline: 1) Delineate your fear, 2) Disown your fear, 3) Display your rear.

The Johnson family will attend the funeral of Susie's former husband who died in Detroit, Michigan, tomorrow.

The Smiths will be leaving for Texas, where Bill will be attached to the hospital post.

"I have shared your FYI—Fear Your Information—column with him."

Pray for Mrs. Smith. She got a good report and the hole is closing.

Blessed are the poot in spirit, for theirs is the kingdom of heaven.

An omitted "g" in a Lenten worship folder changed the theological slant of the call to worship.
Preacher: "Clothe your ministers with righteousness."
People: "Let us sin with joy!"

Barbara C. remains in the hospital and needs blood donors for more transfusions. She is also having trouble sleeping and requests tapes of Brother Jack's sermons.

Next week's sermon will be from Bro…. He is a peacher from Florida.

Youth group activities will be gin at 3:00 p.m.

There will be a pot luck dinner shortly after services today. Be prepared to eat 10-15.

Let's all be reminded to check the sick-up date sheet. (Instead of the sick up-date sheet.)

This evening's songs will be taken from the Scared Collection Hymnal. (Sacred)

Everyone, please check your meekly (weekly) reminder for duties.

The "Over 60's choir" will be disbanded for the summer with the thanks of the entire church.

Pray daily that the Holy Sprit will bless you.

The men's fellowship breakfast will meet Tuesday at 12 sharp.

He that believes in Him shall have ever laughing life.

"Cod be with you."

"Sinday's sermon will be announced later."

Next Thursday there will be tryouts for the choir. They need all the help they can get.

"Be sure to attend the Wednesday Evening Lardies Fellowship."

"By the way, for those of you that have children and don't know it, we have a nursery in the basement of the building."

"The new organ has 29 ranks, and 1800 popes."

Holy Saturday—Easter Vigil—7:30 PM
Easier Festival Service—10:30 AM

"Anyone not at the church parking lot by noon will be executed."

"Be sure to attend the church bizarre."

The meeting was called to order…the agenda was adopted…the minutes were approved…the financial secretary gave the grief report.

The sentence reporting on a guest preacher for an anniversary service read: "The great preacher for the day was a former pastor."

The "Vinegar Bible" (Oxford, 1716-17) substituted "vinegar" for "vineyard" in Luke 22:9.

The "Wife-Hater Bible" (Oxford, 1810) where Luke13:26 came out "If any man come to Me and hate…his own wife (life) also, he cannot be My disciple."

Another MARRIAGE ENCOUNTER weekend is being offered. It's a chance for a weekend away for just you and your souse.

"Whom the Lord loves, he chases."

Song #668 When We Meet in Tweet Communion

Song #663 To Go Be The Glory

On Sunday nights we sometimes had a "Sing-a-long." My bulletin typist omitted one letter in the announcement that left it saying, "7 p.m. tonight, Sin-a-long with Stan."

Sermon topic—"The Washing of Hands: Commentary on hind washing."

Hymn #228—"Jesus Lies, and So Shall I"

This Easter Sunday bulletin caused worshippers to smile. Sunday Sermon: "The Greatest News Ever!" Monday: Pastor's Day Off.

"We hope there will be good attendance for this suspicious occasion."

This particular October events calendar listed: Barker/Renewal of Wedding Vowels.

"Pastor is on vacation, massages can be given to church secretary."

The offertory hymn "Take My Life" was listed as "Table My Life."

"We have exceptional well-brained pastor."

The closing hymn was listed as, "Jesus, Priceless Pressure."

A congregation with Swedish heritage listed the hymn, "Amazing Grace, How Swede the Sound."

"The Odor of Worship is as follows."

One student may have said more than he meant when he wrote about the Apostles Creed, that he believed in "one holy chaotic church."

One boy spoke of baptism by saying, "Unlike the Baptists who believe in total erosion, we Lutherans believe...."

A newspaper's ad carrying an advance notice about a well-known speaker may have promised too much. It ended with "A brief business meeting and conversion with the speaker is planned."

The announcement for our church picnic was supposed to urge people to arrive in informal clothing. It read, "Everyone is asked to wear clothing for the picnic."

Someone had called the bakery to order a cake inscribed, "Happy Birthday, Pastor Bock." As the chaplain entered the lounge, he was startled to see the frosting read, "Happy Birthday, Pass the Buck."

In our church, to aid in the process of welcoming guests, we have ushers quickly fill out information cards as they seat them. One Sunday, the pastor warmly greeted "Lt. Col. Red Mercedes."
Everyone soon realized that the usher, using certain abbreviations had been trying to tell the pastor there was a "light-colored red Mercedes" with lights on in the parking lot.

Computer printouts have added bright spots to our church's business meetings. The account description column is limited to relatively few spaces. Last month in approving the purchase of a license, we approved an item which read, "Food Handler's Lice—$600."

Our church newsletter advertised a men's fishing retreat weekend complete with cabins, boatslips, lake, and lodge for $25.00 a reservation. The date for the weekend was listed as "March 30-June 1."

Our newsletter introduced a new member this way. "I want you to meet Patsy _____, who is a champion swinger."

After being invited over for Sunday lunch, our pastor ended the service with "May the Lord look upon you with flavor and give you peace."

Our new pastor is the Rev. Rebecca Ebb. Our bulletin read, "Please indicate the areas of ministry you could help in and return this form to a member of the committee or Pastor Egg."

A letter which ran in a bulletin explained how the Lutheran Church in America distributes gifts for natural disaster relief. It read, "Natural disasters within the United States are coordinated by the Division for Missions in North America."

Penny _____ begins her internship in the King Country Prosecutor's Office this week. Please remember the Prosecutor's Office in your prayers."

"We welcome the Rev. Howard Kuhnie as our gust speaker."

"We give a haughty welcome to the Rev. LeRoy _____, who will bring us our lesson today."

"If you have not yet received the information, please sue the pastor."

This bulletin announced the full barbecue with these words, "Bring something for yourself and someone else to BBQ."

The closing song will be "Prince of Peach, Control my Will."

"Many items have been left in the church during the past several weeks, including hates, gloves, umbrellas, and coats."

This fund-raising package was addressed to "Holy Gross Lutheran Youth Group" instead of "Holy Cross."

Our secretary must have been thinking of an upcoming event in the King County, Washington, domed stadium when she typed in the Sunday bulletin, "The Kingdome of God."

"LUTHERAN PERISH Worker Wanted."

"The original sin in the new office was too small so a larger one was purchased and installed."

"SELECTION COMMITTEE meets Wednesday,7 p.m., in the Bride's Room."

"The church women are planning an 'English Tea Party,' inviting the women of area Lutheran churches. All women are asked to wear hats and gloves; no slacks please.

"There will not be a covered dish dinner on December 10. Pans have been changed."

"Salvation Army would appreciate receiving canned or boxed groceries, good used sweaters and good used boys for their Christmas assistance program."

"December 9. Christmas Shopping Trip—If you are planning to attend, please sign on your Worship Resister Card."

"Christmas luncheon at the Quality Inn. Lunch at 12:30. Bring an unwrapped gift or man or lady."

"The Service of the Word for Healing, which was canceled due to pastor's illness, has been rescheduled."

"The Christmas decorating party for church starts Sunday at 2 p.m. Bring your saws to cut trees and willing hands."

"Grace Lutheran Church is looking for a 4-year-old preschool teacher."

"Mid week services are still focusing on the Seven Deadly Sins. This week 'Greed and Gluttony.' Join us for services at 7:30, and come earlier for soup and salad at 6:30."

During the dedication of our new public-address system, one of the congregational responses in the bulletin was, "God bless our sound reproduction facilities!"

"We will be having only one service this summer beginning at 9 a.m. June 5, continuing through September 15."

"Then we are mindful that we always live as recipients of God's underserved love."

OFFERING ANTHEM: "Give It Away."

"Flavorable comments were made concerning the use of a loaf of bread instead of wafers for communion."

"Each Wednesday during Advent, the congregation will gather for prayer, medication, and preparation."

"A prerequisite of choir this year is that you must attend ¾ of the rehearsals in order to sin."

Our Savior Lutheran Church, recently received an envelope addressed to: "OUR SURVIVOR'S LUTHERAN CHURCH."

As the coffin was lifted and carried to the altar, more than 3,000 mourners sang the hymn, "O God Our Health and Age Has Past."

"Beverages and dessert are furnished by the Boars of Parish Education."

"In order that a pastor of this congregation may be devoted to the duties of the office, an adequate salary shall be provided, pain in semi-monthly or monthly installments."

"Shepherd singles have their regular monthly meeting Monday at 9:30. Come and share a cup of coffee, roll and fellowship with other single ladies."

"Council Report—Due to the length of the Parish Council meeting, very little business was conducted."

Army chapel bulletin: "Those interested in sinning in the Reformation service chorus, join us for rehearsal Thursday evening."

"This Sunday is Food Bank Sunday. Please remember your donations to Interfaith Ministries to help elevate hunger in our community."

"Baptismal bonnets on hand are: 3 girls, 1 boy. There are 4 boys in the process of being made."

"Bishop calls for peach in Nambia."

"Needed (food pantry) items are: canned juices, canned vegetables, fruits, meats, macaroni diapers, shampoo, tea,…."

"KIDS OF THE KINGDOM will going bowling next Sunday. Cost includes 2 games bowling, shoes, pizza, and pot."

"90% of ELCA churches have one or fewer families."

"I will cling to the old rugged cross/and exchange it some day for a crow."

"Organ recital of Lenten music at the Park Church, with linch following, if you desire."

"Baptismal Hymn: I Was There To Hear Your Boring Cry."

"We would like members to write down their favorite hymns and drip them in the offering plate."

"Men should be freshly shaved for the pictorial directory, except for the bearded variety and those with mustaches."

"Lunch will be served following the burial in the church basement."

"The bouquet of flowers is from their children and they are in the bowl from their 40th wedding anniversary."

"St. John's has been asked to donate the following items to the Junior High Camp…4 dozen homemade cookies or candy bras."

"Sunday we will hold a service…at which we will also install our new and old leadership and deceive new members."

"7:30 a.m. Jr. Choir's trip to Noah's Ark. Rain date is June 27."

"SERMON: 'How to burn without burning out'…Pastor Wick."

"Next Sunday's Forum will deal with the subject of cremation. The guest speaker will be Mike Ashburn."

"March 21, 7:30 p.m.—Worship followed by coffee. 'Weak Yet Strong' Compassion."

"Lenten Service with the St. Jacob players resenting the play, 'NO NAME STREET.'"

"Building money will be used for insulting the west wall of the fellowship hall."

"Friday: Church Women United—Retreat at Our Lady of the Mountain."

"We want to sing our favorite hymns this summer. You can help by listing three hums from the hymnal and put your name below."

Our church's Easter breakfast was advertised as "No Resurrection Necessary" to be admitted.

"Holy Communion will be served on the first Sunday, on Maundy Thursday, and on Eater Sunday."

"Let us confess our sin to God…who has promised to forgive and cleanse us from all nutritiousness."

"…your old men shall dream reams, and your young men shall see visions."

"In conjunction with the annual meeting, a lunch persisting of spaghetti and meatballs will be served."

A letter to Rev. John E. Priest said, "Dear Pastor Priest."

"Rachel Circle will resume their meetings on January 27. Call ladies of the church are invited."

"Please greet the newest embers in the Fellowship Hall."

"The men's group will hold their annual meeting. The offering will be taken for the Salvation Army. Bring your wife!"

"God never gives us more than we can bare."

"Saturday activities include special interest groups (self worth, single parent families, the treat of legal gambling, spouse abuse…)"

"Pastor Kutson was elected bishop and with him goes the hopes, prayers, and dreams of a synod."

"Thanks to all those who shared all those beautiful Poinsettia pants with the congregation during the holidays."

"An oyster or children dinner is available between 1 and 5:30."

Church camp announcement: "Be a cool dud and come to Camp Shep."

Meeting topic: "Women's rule in the church."

4:30 p.m.—SMORGASBORD
6:30 p.m.—Suicide Survivors Support Group.

GIFTS AND MEMORIALS: $400 for Elevator Fun given by Helen.

"Before the lecture he will be discussing his personal faith struggle in suffering at a potluck dinner."

"Following the meeting they will go out and pick up their section of Hwy 34."

"Singles on the church roof were checked out. We have some on hand and will replace them next spring."

"L. W. will pray for weeds in the parking lot and sidewalks."

"Thanks for sending me the material on the hot for profit housing corporation you are forming."

"Hymn of the day—Give To Our God Immoral Praise."

"People over 60, please visit our Senior Center. Males daily, programs, bus trips year round."

Church Council Minutes Summary, "Exterminator took on the ant problem. One year warranty. Inactive members being contacted."

"The men not only helped set up, but also cooked the children and cleaned up after!"

The 1991 Spring Council Retreat will be hell May 10 and 11.

"A group has been formed to help stagnate churches."

This church sent this notice of its congregational meeting "to decide questions concerning the furnace and the pastoral call."

"7 p.m.: Pre-Martial Workshop and Wedding Service."

The Extension office will present a program on premenstrual syndrome and how it affects women at St. Matthew Lutheran Church.

"Please bring an offering and a snake to share."

"LSS FOOD PANTRY needs food. Michelle _____, who runs the pantry, has fun out of money to buy food."

"There will not be a Week of Prayer for United Service next Sunday, due to schedule conflicts for five of the six congregations involved."

"You, as a spiritual leader in Sacramento, are encouraged to attend, be robbed, and participate in the procession."

"Easter Sunrise Service, Sunday, 6 p.m."

Fund raiser for the Benefit Floor breakfast: "So plan now to eat breakfast at the church, make a contribution, and then see your results on the floor."

Treasurer's Report: "We finally took in more for the year than we spent, even with the once-a-year insurance bull of $2,653."

The final Lenten Service theme is: "Why Doesn't God Do Something?" with Pastor Meidinger.

On the church kitchen bulletin board: "Egg Dippers—Make Sure You Cover Your Bottoms!" (Posted after complaints that some of the Easter eggs bottoms weren't covered with chocolate.)

"The correspondence committee will assist with the mailing of the newsletter and stapling of the Annual Report to congregational members."

Musician Wanted: "Must be able to play piano in Spanish for two services."

"Organ recital on Sunday at 3 p.m. Mark your calendar for two services."

"Midnight Mass will begin at 10 p.m."

"Start saving your aluminum cans and bring them to church on Sunday. If you cannot get your cans to church, contact any youth group member to help you."

"The pastor's class for prospective members and other inquirers will meet Sundays in the conference room of the lover level."

"Confirmation classes will be held the second and fourth Sundays of each week."

"Bring potluck dish and drink to share. Hot dogs, hamburgers, and children will be provided as well as paper products."

"What 'ere we do for thin/O Lord, we do it unto thee."

Item for sale: "Used church lights. Contact pastor during the day."

"World Hugger Sunday—Special world hunger offering opportunity."

A local restaurant included on its Sunday menu: "Baked Fillet of Soul."

"Scavenger Hung to help the Food Pantry."

"Moving the church lawn this week will be Allen _____ and Roland _____."

The teacher training workshop promotes the featured speaker as "recognized for expertise ineffective instruction."

"There will be tables on the porch outside the narthex to answer questions and to purchase Bibles."

We will be having a reception after the service. Libby _____ is coordinating persons to bake cakes and kitchenworkers."

Pastor Brent _____, Pianist Jane _____, Greeters the Brown Family, Users Jack and June Smith.

In our church there is an "over 50's" group that calls itself the "Gold Group." In the bulletin it was announced, "The Old Group will have its fellowship Wednesday night."

"There will be a vandalism committee meeting Sunday after services."

"With 60 faulty members, it is the largest seminary in the world."

Communion instructions in this church read: "Communicants will receive the host, then dip it into the wind, and return to the pew."

A Palm Sunday bulletin read: "The palm branches will be collected as you leave to be burned."

For the coffee hour, the announcement read, "The Heinz family is furnishing threats this morning."

As our new church was being built, our pastor reassured us in his newsletter that, "The survivors are outside lining up the angels for the new building."

Our social service committee was conducting its quarterly blood pressure clinic, causing someone to put up this sign in front of the church: "Blood pressure taken in rear."

The member who was supposed to be both lector and offering counter became ill, and the pastor left me this note. "Nancy is sick—can't read or count." It made me wonder what kind of sickness was involved.

The ad for a Lutheran College President asked applicants to send curriculum and vitae and the names of "three referees."

Our congregation was planning an adult class for those considering the church for membership. The classes were advertised as primarily for those of other "demoninational" backgrounds.

A synod pastor was hospitalized with a broken kneecap. A typo with the newsletter notice seemed curiously appropriate. It read, "Your remembrances and cars will be appreciated."

"Our picture gallery is being slowly updated by Gary _____. Please cooperate when he approaches you to be shot.

"You are invited to greet Bishop Chilstrom at a reception in his honor…and to worship him at Evening Prayer, 5:30 p.m.

This church has apparently found a way to measure the impact of its sermons. It recently announced "Blood pressure screening before and after the service."

Our church's handbook listed projects for each circle. Due to an error, one project called for the repair of "humans" instead of hymnals.

This church listed among items needed for the food pantry, "port and beans."

Members were reluctant to sign up for a physical fitness program when the announcement read, "Exorcise class."

"The history of this church was going to be dramatized in a unique, most unusual way…"Fellowship hour with display of guilts by women of St. Matthias Church."

A lot of research evidently goes into site location for synod offices. An official memorandum states that the best choice for offices would be at Trinity Church, Tacoma, because it's "located where Lutherans are most dense."

The sermon topic was announced in the bulletin as "Too Much Noise," with "Pastor Bang preaching."

"Thank you Dick ___ who once again has worked hard to clean the pastor off the basement floor."

John 8:32: "And you shall know the truth, and the truth shall make you mad."

Preparation for Lent included the traditional Shrove Tuesday supper. In the monthly church calendar the invitation read: "Shove Dinner with Service."

"Let goods and kindred go, thy moral life also…."

"Ushers will eat latecomers at these points."

"There will be waxers and stripers available for the Men's Club when they do the fellowship hall floor."

"The Lutheran men's group will meet at 6 p.m. Steak, mashed potatoes, green beans, bread, and dessert will be served for a nominal feel."

"There will be a congregational meeting after worship service…to approve the budget for 1989. Please plan not to attend."

"We are having a church blood drive. The soup and sandwich lunch is available for those who give blood and their families."

"Craig ___ is working on the plaque for piano fund donors."

THE HYMN: "I've Got a Robe, You've Got a Rob."

"Come and celebrate! Pastor Steve will present his last sermon on Sunday."

FOOD PANTY PROGRAM meets emergency food needs for 6-10 families per week.

"Our sanctuary is now air-conditioned for the summer months and is cooking our summer worshippers."

"Our best wishes are extended to Gene and Joan who were yesterday untied in Christian marriage."

In an Army base church bulletin: "Jesus Jeep Me Near the Cross."

"Ricky, Rachel, and Norma are workers on the bus ministry. On Sunday morning they can be seen busy at work in the Fellowship Building mixing and pouring drinks for the Sunday school children."

"Yes, I would like to sin with the choir June 12."

"Do This in Remembrance of Me" is the title of...a special memorial ceremony for members who have died during the past two years at both services."

While welcoming guests and visitors to Sunday morning worship, our bulletin that should have said how "tickled" we were for their presence, read: "We're really ticked that you are here."

"The senior choir invites any member of the congregation who enjoys sinning to join the choir."

"Please join us as we show our support for Amy and Alan in preparing for the girth of their first child."

"Surely He Has Bourne Our Briefs."

"The Tired Sunday in Advent."

"Remember in prayer the many who are sick of our community."

"If you received a Christmas fruit basket from Augustana, if possible, return it to the church by next November."

"Spend one Sunday each week at your nearest church."

"Please do not immerse the coffee servers."

"Let me be thin forever."

"A nursery is provided at all services, and interpretation for the hearing available at the 10:00 service."

A church project announcement said, "A trailer from Don ___ will be sued for cleaning potatoes as needed."

"BALONY CLASS" The Balcony Sunday school class is beginning a new unit of study.

"Our Witness Commission is sponsoring a dull-color church directory to help us match names to faces."

"SOMETHING TO GIVE THANKS FOR: Both Les and Rachael were involved in very serious accidents in which the vehicles they were riding were totally destroyed. Thanks be to God."

"The evening service was assigned for those with hearing impairments, and liturgical dancers stimulated the senses in yet another way."

"The first month's men's breakfast was held Saturday and was a huge success. Those present missed a lot!"

"The prayers of the church are asked for Mary, Caroline, and Jacob, who are in need of God's helling grace."

"There will be plenty of room in the oven for those people who bring a hot dish to the church service before the dinner."

"Any monies not raised through the sale of the Organ Certificates will be borrowed eternally."

"Children will be given sermon-related bulleting by the ushers for the use during worship service.

"Fiends at Zion wish you God's blessings at this happy time."

"Eight new black choir robes are currently needed, due to the addition of several new members and to the deterioration of some older ones."

"This church will dedicate four works of art in memory of eight persons who have died over the past several years at the conclusion of the 9:30 worship service Sunday."

"Scouts are saving aluminum cans, bottles and other items to be recycled. Proceeds will be used to cripple children."

"First communion classes will begin on Sunday at 9:45….If interested, please Pastor Wittcopp."

This letter to the church concluded, "Gold bless your thoughts and actions."

"Perhaps envelopes need to be stuffed with senior volunteers for a congregational mailing."

"Lent provides addictional opportunities for worship and prayer."

"The youth are selling delicious frozen pies to raise funds for their Dallas trip. You may see them after services today, or expect a call from one."

This bulletin read, "Ladies of the Evening" Circle will meet at 7:30 tonight. I didn't really know what to think because I was a visitor to this church. As I kept reading, though, it became more apparent. It was just differentiating this group from the Morning and Afternoon Circles.

Weight Watchers will meet at 7 p.m. at the First Presbyterian Church. Please use the large double door at the side entrance.

Housing Needed. We are seeking volunteers to host members of the Clare College Choir for the evening of Monday, September 13th. If you have some extra room and would like to hose two or three of these college age students from Cambridge, England, please call Sue.

While I lay wrapped in sleep and unconscious of myself, Your sleepless eye kept vigil.

"We will dedicate our new restroom facilities with the singing of, "Great God, A Blessing From Thy Throne."

Church bulletin: ORDER OR WORSHIP ("Well, OK, I'll have a cheeseburger to go.")

"Area local concerns and panty donations were approved to be given to the Interfaith Community Pantry."

Needed: Love seat for counseling center.

As we bring this child through baptism into the Kongdom of God…

Area panty donations were approved.

We invite everyone to the insulation service for the new pastor.

Don't forget the potluck after services. Bring your foot and put it on the center table.

The preacher training workshop promotes the featured speaker as "recognized for expertise ineffective instruction."

The topic for the Elders' Bible Class will be "Sinplicity of Christianity."

Those interested sinning in the Reformation service chorus, join us for rehearsal.

Sermon: "Biting off more than you can chew." Communion Hymn: "Let Us Break Bread Together."

We extend a welm warcome to everyone.

If anyone has additional input, please give it to the elders in the rear.

"Everyone helping with the used clothing round-up will be heaving a pot luck."

"A most sincere thank you to everyone for all the cards, prayers, and words of encouragement during my illness and death."

Don't let worry kill you off. Let the church help."

"Potluck supper: prayer and medication will follow."

"The number of nursery volunteers has been swindling."

The bulletin made reference to I Corinthians 13, which reads "Love never faileth." Unfortunately, the proofreader goofed and the passage read "Lover never faileth."

The bulletin informed us that our church would be sending an important questionnaire to the homes of all members. "The survey will as the congregation..."

Michael and Deborah were married on October 24 in the church. So ends a friendship that began in school days.

"Miss Mable Johnson will be entering the hospital this week for 'testes'."

"The Mary Magdalene Project is a residential program for women wanting to leave prostitution supported by Presbyterians."

Pastor John will deliver the Advent massage.

Anthen: How Lovely is Thy Swelling Place.

Communion Motel (instead of Motet)

Pastor Mike will deliver the message. A special sining and dinner will follow.

"The Magic of Lassie," a film for the whole family, will be shown Sunday at 5 p.m. in the church hall. Free puppies to all children not accompanied by parents.

"Tickets for the drawing can be purchased as you pass out after services."

The closing prayer included, "…may we workshop you in spirit and truth."

"The Women's Evening Circle will meet on Tuesday. All men are invited for fun and fellowship."

SPECIAL THANKS To all teachers, music leaders, servers, children and our ladies group (Christmas bags).

Music for Advent…Chancel Choir with Bras Ensemble.

"We invite you and your wife for a wonderful baked ham dinner followed by an evening of sinning."

One church sent out a notice of its congregational meeting "to decide questions concerning the furnace and the pastoral call."

"Sermon title: 'The Devil Speaks.' Pastor Bill will be giving the sermon."

From the minutes of a church council meeting: "The pulpit loudspeaker system was discussed; there have been complaints of being able to hear the sermon."

"Come and celebrate! Pastor Steve will present his last sermon on Sunday."

Messages on a church signboard:
> PASTOR BOB IS ON VACATION. PRAISE THE LORD!

SUNDAY MORNING SERMON: "JESUS WALKING ON WATER."
SUNDAY EVENING SERMON: "LOOKING FOR JESUS."

"Please note in your church directory the Lord's new address (the phone number will remain the same)." The Lord family had bought a new house.

This notice was left on the door for the Hispanic custodian of a California church: "Dear Jesus—Please buff the floor and lock up when you leave."

"Don't let worry kill you off. Let the church help."

"Remember in prayer the many who are sick of our church and community."

"The outreach committee has enlisted twenty-five volunteers to make calls on people who are not afflicted with any church."

As the coffin was lifted and carried to the altar, more than three thousand mourners sang the hymn, "O God, Our Health and Age Has Past."

"We offer prayers of thanksgiving on behalf of Jeremy W., who has been experiencing health problems. He has undergone a recent brain scan, and they didn't find anything."

"Helen White has been taken seriously. She is in Memorial Hospital."

In my hometown newspaper one day, the obituaries ran in column one and the funeral notices were in column four on the same page. I found it amusing that sandwiched between these somber columns the newspaper had run a huge ad stating "*News-Times*—the newspaper that wakes up the city!"

When the church becomes a business…Organ prelude: "Jesus, Priceless Treasure."

Next hymn: "Jesus Paid It All $156" (instead of #156).

Hymn #67: "Away in a Manger."

Offeratory: "Steal Away."

"Council Report—Due to the length of the Parish Council meeting very little business was conducted."

"Sunday we will hold a service at which we will also install our new and old leadership and deceive new members."

"Jane Elliot, president, opened the meeting with a poem. The Lord's Prayer was then read and approved."

"Before the lecture he will be discussing his personal faith struggle in suffering at a potluck dinner."

"The Junior Ladies' Guild will have a benefit luncheon on Sunday. They will be serving the same wonderful meal they served last year."

"Cheerfulness promotes health and immorality."

A church secretary wrote that she thankfully caught this error before the bulletin was printed: "Pastor John will deliver the Advent massage."

"Gifts and Memorials: $40 for Elevator Fun given by Helen."

"There will be a baby shower for Rachel Hanson, expecting twins today, Nov. 2, from 2-4."

Muscular Christianity: "Following the meeting they will go out and pick up their section of Hwy. 34."

The radio hostess was talking about the importance of Christian music in our lives. She said, "Christian music has always been part of our Christian heresy."

"George Butler's name was intentionally omitted from the list of Sunday school teachers."

Male and female he created them…
Meeting topic: "Women's rule in the church."

"Hymn #234: Wise Up, O Men of God."

"The Salvation Army would appreciate receiving canned or boxed groceries, good used sweaters and good used boys for their Christmas assistance program."

Preparation for Lent included the traditional Shrove Tuesday supper. In the monthly church calendar the invitation read, "Shove Dinner with Service."

The Palm Sunday bulletin read, "The palm branches will be collected as you leave to be burned."

"Children will be given sermon-related bulleting by the ushers for use during the worship service."

Not only that, but…"Ushers will eat latecomers at these points."

"The concert held in the Fellowship Hall was a great success. Special thanks are due to the minister's daughter, who labored the whole evening at the piano, which as usual fell upon her."

"Henrietta Turner will offer a rare vocal threat as she presents a selection of eighteenth-century hymns."

Sing along with…
"Table My life, and Let It Be."

"When We Meet in Tweet Communion."

"Prince of Peach, Control My Will."

"To Go Be the Glory"

"Jesus Lies, and So Shall I"

"A worm welcome to Kathy, our guest organist."

The prelude for June 21 was listed as *Pop and Circumstance*. Appropriately, that Sunday was Father's Day.

During the dedication of the new public-address system, one of the congregational responses in the bulletin read, "God bless our sound reproduction facilities!"

"We have a wonderful time at Wednesday night service, so why come."

The church Execution Board meeting will begin at 7 p.m.

A special thanks to the Ladies Club for the flowers and pants for the pastor.

The fund raising supper will consist of a meat dish with pastor and/or spaghetti sauce. (Pasta).

Sermon: Don't Pay the Water Bill.

Bishop re-elected. Disaster funds raised.

After services there will be a meeting to discuss the nerds of the church.

Trinity's annual Garage & Bake Sale will be held at the garage in the lower lot. No clothes please.

Those who wish to have their marriage vows removed may come forward at this time.

Most religions try to keep God in the realm of timeless immorality.

Pastor will address the practical points of fasting. The Anders family will bring doughnuts for all.

Veiling of the Cross—Pastor Bill drapes the Cross with Pastor Terry.

Red balloons will be released containing confirmands.

Our guest speaker next week has pestered numerous churches over the years.

PLEASE—Do not throw rice or bird seed at the wedding coupe. They will eat it, swell and blow up if you do.

Our church is proud to participate in the "Scared Places Tour," sponsored by the Historical Society.

We need help supplying threats at the Youth Rally.

Two chaperones are needed for the Synod Youth Fathering.

Eight members of the church baked or served 96 people at the Soup Supper.

The church support has swindled to less than 24%

The Youth Group will meet Wednesday evening at 7. It will last about one year.

Psalm 112 (Read responsibly.)

The bathroom and kitchen plumbing has been modified, so the possibility of children being scolded has been eliminated.

We have a new member. She has been loving in a motel until she can rent an apartment.

We are truly blessed with our ministries. All the broads have done an excellent job.

Article in USA TODAY referred to the Martini Lutheran Church in Baltimore.

TOYS FOR TOOTS—Donations appreciated.

There will be a large selection of Christmas coolies.

Hymn—Hark the Herald Angels Sin.

The Fire Department ruled that there is no regulation to prevent hand-held candles as long as they are not unattended.

Are we ready to join the angels as they sin?

Please sign up on the sheep located in the auditorium.

Nametags are stored apathetically in the foyer.

Please remember to bring non-perishable food and diaper donations.

No gum chewing or eating the chapel.

Sisters in the Lord is sharing God's love and men at Reformation.

Program will be by the pastor's wives.

A swill steak supper will be served from 5-7.

The Evangelical Lutheran Church of Saint Phillip—Afflicted with the Missouri Synod.

Pastors who were called to Glory—None as of this printing.

Given in memory of charter members who have died by Mr. & Mrs. Toxin.

Confirmation class will study adultery with Pastor David.

The state of Michigan tested our water today. It's good except for the taste.

New organist looking for someone to play with.

Sin during offering.

Just As I am Without One Pea.

Electric chair available for the asking.

Wanted: Nutsery School teacher.

Children cause disruptions. Please do not hesitate to send a child out until he or she can be composted.

On the way to church, pick up an individual or tow.

Be sure to pick up your Satan Angels. (Satin)

The Jacobsens are hosting a co-ed shower for Cindy in Room 205.

From deep within my heart I would like to say thank you each and every one who so generously gave hugs, money and such a nice diner in my honor.

Surely he has born our briefs.

After reading this ad in our paper, I wondered what kind of problems the local church had: "Beautiful home site—5 to 13 acres. Features included running creek, wooded hills and fenced pastor."

Anyone not wanting to drive his or her car to the songfest, meet in the parking lot where we can car poop.

The altar flowers are in loving memory of Herman S., who was called to his heavenly home by his wife.

Twenty-two members were present at the church meeting held in the home of Mrs. Marsha C. last evening. Mrs. C. and Mrs. R. sang a duet, The Lord Knows Why.

A songfest was hell at the Methodist church Wednesday.

Today's sermon: HOW MUCH CAN A MAN DRINK? With hymns from a full choir.

The pastor will preach his farewell message, after which the choir will sing, "Break Forth into Joy."

During the absence of our pastor, we enjoyed the rare privilege of hearing a good sermon when Pastor Stubbs supplied our pulpit.

Next Sunday Mrs. V. will be soloist for the morning service. The pastor will then speak on, "It's a Terrible Experience."

The 8th graders will be presenting Shakespeare's Hamlet in the church basement on Friday at 7 p.m. The congregation is invited to attend this tragedy.

Sermon Title, "The Devil Speaks." Pastor Bill will be giving the sermon.

A few years ago the Reverend Ron Christ was called to the Presbyterian Church of Sidney, Iowa. The banner headline in the local paper read, "Christ comes to Sidney."

A small, white girl's bicycle was found in the church's parking lot. (Another comma should have followed the word "white").

BURNING BOWL SERVICE: January 5, 2 p.m. During the burning bowel service you are given the opportunity to let go and release anything unwanted in your life.

The Rev. Adams spoke briefly, much to the delight of his audience.

Frank A. suffered a heat stroke Saturday and is in the hospital. He was delirious in the emergency room and it took three nurses to seduce him. (Sedate)

The Ladies Liturgy Society will meet on Wednesday. Mrs. Johnson will sing "Put Me in my Little Bed," accompanied by the pastor.

Christmas Sinspiration and special music.

We rejoice and give thanks that the family got out safely and no one was insured.

Many hunger for a slice of bread or a simple bowel of soup.

A cycle of medications for Epiphany.

The men will have their annual Ground Hog sausage and pancakes February 2.

A sin up sheet is available in the narthex.

The congregation may strip while the altar is being seated.

Scripture: Filipinos 2:5-11.

On two adjacent lines:
Sermon: "On the night in which He was betrayed."
No soup supper.

Those children who have taken special instruction will receive both elements (bread and wind).

There were no deaths in the past month. Betty and Jackie are scheduled for May. (They were in charge of funeral luncheons.)

We ask your help if you play an instrument, sin or do liturgical dance.

If you are going through a difficult time and need a fiend, let us know.

Let angels prostate fall.

Chancel flowers in honor of their 16th wedding by Bob and Barb.

The Christmas Corral will be at the Holy Rosary Catholic church.

The pastor will light the ushers and they will in turn light the congregation.

I'd rather help a little child
To over come his rear,
Then to be a hero in a book,
Tho lauded far and near.

On Sunday, a special collection will be taken to defray the expenses of the new carpet. All wishing to do something on the new carpet, come forward and get a piece of paper.

Please pray for Barbara P. at her ordination, and all others who are ill or suffering.

From a California church: Today we welcome Cody V. into the family of God in the Sacramento of Holy Baptism.

Bring one dozen bookies to the Nov. 9 meeting.

Junior High Fun Night: Bring a friend and/or hot dog and marshmallows to roast.

Friends raised at the breakfast will be sent to one of the congregations for use in the earthquake disaster.

Sermon: The Biggest Fish Story of All
Hymn: I Love to Tell the Story.

Mainline Protestant denominations are in danger of extinction at the unit's October board meeting.

Be sure to come to the Benefit Pig Roast for the Bacon family.

Pastor John will deliver a short sermon on the subject of reducing violence at the close of the worship service.

Choir Robbing Room.

First Lutheran's potluck gets carried away.

We will remember those who died during communion.

Two signs on a post: One Way (with arrow pointing to the right) Lutheran Church (with arrow to the left).

The purpose of this party is to fester Christian fellowship and fun.

A special thanks to our college group who backed over 200 cookies for the Christmas bags.

The Community Festival Choir will present experts from Handel's Messiah today at 2 p.m.

The third verse of "Blessed Assurance" will be sung without musical accomplishment.

Smile at someone who his hard to love. Say "hell" to someone who doesn't know you.

Miss Mason sang, "I will not Pass this Way Again," giving obviously pleasure to the congregation.

Next Sunday is the family hay ride and bonfire at the Fowlers. Bring your own hot dogs and guns. Friends are welcome! Everyone come for a fun time.

Easter Sunday we will have a 9:30 worship service. The 11:00 will be hell as usual.

Missionary from Africa speaking at Calvary Memorial Church in Racine—Name: Bertha Belch. Come tonight and hear Birtha Belch all the way from Africa.

Announcement in the church bulletin for a conference: The cost for attending the National Fasting & Prayer Conference includes meals.

Our youth basketball team is back in action Wednesday at 8 p.m. in the rec. hall. Come and watch us beat Christ the King!

Our next song is "Angels We Have Heard Get High."

Jean will be leading a weight management series Wednesday nights. She's used the program herself and has been growing like crazy!

"Take my vice and let me sing."

The youth group meeting was canceled and the bulletin read:
NO GOOD NEWS
CLUB TONIGHT.

We were supposed to have a hymn out of the "Sing and Celebrate" hymnal, but the bulletin said "Sin and Celebrate" hymnal.

4

Miscellaneous Bloopers

Martha, the custodian at church, is a real tyrant. Everyone fears her wrath, including the pastor. No one dares to track in dirt, rearrange the hymnals, or do anything else without securing her approval. One day my daughter was telling me what she wanted to be when she grew up. "I want to be a pastor, Mom," she said. I regretfully told her that our church doesn't allow female pastors. She then decided she would be an elder. "Nope, no female elders allowed either," I said.

She was silent and thoughtful for a minute, then brightened and exclaimed, "Okay, then I'll be a custodian like Martha. She runs the church anyway."

After several weeks of extremely hot summer weather, the sign in the church yard read, "And You Think THIS Is Hot!"

Bumper sticker: "I'm laying my treasures up in heaven…just look at my car."

Another bumper sticker: "Trust in God—She will provide."

Sign on the door of a Hong Kong dentist: "Teeth extracted by latest Methodists."

I sell handmade Christmas ornaments at craft shows. One day an elderly nun bought two children's ornaments from me. I asked her, "Are those for your grandchildren?" Oops.

A few years ago I was minister of music in a Baptist church in Stockton, California. One day when the pastor was out, the fire marshal, along with a couple of firefighters, came by the church to do a fire safety inspection. At the conclusion of the inspection they gave me a verbal report. One of the firemen, making reference to the baptistry, said, in all sincerity, "Oh, by the way, you got some crickets in your hot tub."

My aunt an uncle arrived late at the family reunion. They'd had a special service at church, followed by two guest speakers. My uncle commented that the speakers were interesting, but the morning had certainly gone on too long. "After all," he said mischievously, "The mind can only absorb as long as the rear can endure."

While I was listening to a radio broadcast of a church service, the station went off the air. About a minute or two later it came back on and the radio announcer said, "Due to circumstances beyond our control, we will now return you to the worship service."

The song leader had just gotten new glasses. He walked up to the podium without his glasses and announced that the next song would be "Standing on the Promises," on page 502. He got the page number correct, but it was not the song he mentioned. When the congregation began to chuckle, he put on his glasses and discovered his error. On page 502 the song "Open Mine Eyes, That I Might See." He grinned and said, "Maybe if I would open mine eyes I would get it right."

I was flipping through the TV channels rather quickly and stopped at one that had a minister praying. His eyes were closed, his forehead furrowed, and he looked to be in deep conversation with God. My wife asked me what channel that was, and I told her, 'That's the blind channel." She remarked that she didn't know there was a special channel for the blind, but thought it was a good idea.

Over the massive front doors of a church, these words were inscribed: "The Gates of Heaven." Below that was a small cardboard sign that read, "Please use other entrance."

I'm the principal of a small Christian elementary school. One morning before school, I visited the cook in the kitchen and was horrified when she told me she'd seen a big rat. "It even sat up and looked at me before it ran away and hid!" She exclaimed. She related that she'd called her husband and he had already managed to kill and remove the rat.

Unfortunately, my relief was short-lived. Thirty minutes later at our morning chapel service, I got a sick feeling in my stomach when our fifth-grade teacher made the announcement that their class hamster had escaped during the night. Sometimes I hate this job!

Our youngest daughter is a natural teacher and loves being with young children. One year during high school and for the entire year, we would enter the church to a chorus of young whispered voices saying, "There's Angie!" "Mom, Dad, it's Angie!" "Look, there's my Sunday school teacher, Angie!" It was a bit humbling to be known as the Sunday school teacher's dad after I had spent nearly twenty-five years teaching there myself.

As I stood up for the benediction, all four buttons on the back of my dress popped open. A nice male friend of mine gently buttoned them and all was well until after the service when I turned around to thank him and found out it wasn't my friend, but a visitor.

As the newly-immersed Christian climbed out of the baptistery, the stones that were hemmed into the bottom of his baptismal gown fell out onto the steps, which he then stepped on with his bare feet. We could read the thoughts going through his head, and the words he was thinking should have made him a candidate for re-baptizing.

The song director said, "Our final hymn will be 'Take Time to be Holy.'" After checking his watch he added, "In the interest of time, let's sing just he first and last verses."

A former high school teacher of mine was an usher at church one Sunday. He also collected the offering and as he walked past me to pass the collection plate, he bent down to admire my newborn baby that I was holding. He gently pulled black her blanket to take a peek and was mortified to discover that she was nursing.

The song director said, "Due to lack of time, let's just sing every other word of hymn 323."

Our choir director explained that the songs we were singing were called octavos because they had eight pages of music. Someone earnestly asked her what they would be called if there were nine or ten pages instead. A voice from the back row called out, "NINTENDO."

Our church advertised for Easter Service:
Come early for pancake breakfast.
Sermon title: "He's Still Alive!"

One man sang off key so badly it was said that he was inventing new notes.

The men at our church refer to the ladies' group as "Tower of Babel's Club."

On church sign boards:

> Come Early
> Get a Back Seat

> Welcome to Bethel's Church
> Happy Hour 9-10 (It was a kid's service)

> Sermon: No End in Sight

> Sermon:
> The Greatest Sin of All
> Pastor Romstad

BUMPER STICKERS:

> NATIONAL ATHEIST DAY
> APRIL 1

> GET RIGHT
> OR
> GET LEFT
> LIFE IS SHORT
> PRAY HARD!

> THE NEXT TIME YOU THINK YOU'RE PERFECT
> TRY WALKING ON WATER

> WHEN THE LAST TRUMPET SOUNDS,
> I'M OUTTA HERE!

I JOINED A CHURCH WHERE I DIDN'T KNOW A SOUL.
NOW I AM ONE.

Sign next to a church parking lot: DO NOT ENTER

Shortly before the funeral service began, one of the mourners I the front row became ill and had to be escorted out the side door (near the lectern) by two of the pallbearers. The door automatically locked behind them. Soon the minister entered and began his sermon with the words, "We feel God's presence today." Everyone present was startled when a series of knocks resounded in the room. The two pallbearers were locked out and wanted back in.

There was a family whose last name was Church. They had a baby girl whom they named Helen. Thereafter they were accused of "raising Helen Church."

One of the elders lost his regular glasses while canoeing. As he got up to read the church announcements, he put on his prescription sunglasses, looked up from the podium and said, "This looks like a shady group today."

One usher offered to "sew us to our sheets."

At one church, after repair of the drinking fountain, which had long suffered with poor water pressure, the following sign was placed above it:

> If thou presseth too hard upon
> the button, thou shalt be
> reminded of thy baptism.

When I was in high school, I played in the church guitar group. We were seated up front and off to the side in full view of the entire congregation. At the point during the mass when the priest prayed for the recently deceased, he pronounced the deceased parishioner's last name with extra emphasis. As he bellowed "Jane ZITT" our group of young adults fought valiantly to control our giggles. This was a triple whammy as far as inappropriateness of laughter: 1) we were praying, 2) we were up front in full view of everyone, and 3) for goodness' sakes, the poor woman had just died and her family may be been in the congregation!

I attend a small Christian college in Tennessee, where the annual commencement processional hymn was "How Firm a Foundation." By the time the seniors, faculty, choir, speakers, and etc., had marched in, we had sung all the stanzas of the hymn several times. My roommate and many of my friends were members of Vesper Choir—and they HATED that hymn! When I asked why, they replied, "Well, we just get so tired of singing 'Yoo-Hoo' to Jesus." ("You who Jesus has blessed…") Forty-some years later, nobody in my family or among my close friends is able to sing that hymn without smiling.

A funeral director cracks me up in church because he always prays, "Bless us in our undertakings."

During the depression, nothing was wasted. Ladies used flour sacks to make clothing, blankets, etc. One Sunday a rather large woman was being baptized by full immersion. When she exited the baptistery, her white gown became quite transparent and the congregation could clearly read the words "self-rising" on her underwear.

The Catholic church in our small town bought an old parking lot for the site of their new church. The members of the building committee soon had to endure several jokes about installing a drive-through confessional called "Toot 'n Tell."

My daughter and I had made tentative plans to attend the Hot Air Balloon Convention in Albuquerque, New Mexico. At the Ladies Church Group one afternoon a friend asked me if I had any vacations planned for the spring. I told her I was thinking about going to a Hot Air Convention in April. She looked at me strangely and remarked, "Hot Air Convention? You can stay in this room and get plenty of hot air!" I had failed to mention the balloons.

Instead of instructing the choir to sing 'a cappella," the director said, "Everybody sing…'Acapulco.'"

As I was sitting through a mass, the PA system started picking up a prerecorded Lutheran church service that was being broadcast from a nearby radio station. It was really funny because I knew the Lutheran pastor, and that was his voice coming over our speakers. I guess if I believed it was divine intervention I would think I was a member of the wrong faith, but since I work in radio, I know how radio waves can cross over if crystals aren't aligned correctly.

During an immersion baptism, the lady's wig came off when she was under the water. When she surfaced, her wig had rotated 180 degrees.

The choir director was unsure what the name of the anthem was, so he left a "Post-It" note in the blank space for the bulletin secretary. The note said, "I'll call and let you know." He then forgot to call the secretary, so she thought "I'll Call and Let You Know" was the name of the choir anthem and that's how it appeared in Sunday's bulletin.

A lady went to her Pastor and complained that a sex parlor was opening downtown. He thought it odd, but decided to take a look. As he drove by the building in question he saw the sign in the window, "Martial Arts." The lady was sure it said "Marital Arts."

A young crooner turned to the hymn "I Need Thee Every Hour" and whispered to his new girlfriend that it was "their" song. She flipped to another hymn and countered with "God Will Take Care of You.'

My dad would frequently refer to our pastor as "an angel up in the air…harping."

We were watching a TV movie when a woman supposedly was giving birth. I commented that it wasn't very realistic since there was no "Biblical" cord attached to the baby. My husband teasingly replied, "Well, maybe there were problems with the 'Philippian' tubes."

I used to attend a Southern Baptist church where there was a lot of "Praise the Lord!" and "Amen, Reverend!" going on during the sermon. One Sunday a bee stung one of the members and he let out a yelp only to set off a chain reaction of several members shouting "Amen" and "Praise the Lord!"

My son came home from Mass with this joke: "What do you get when you mix holy water and prune juice? A religious movement!"

Attention Catholic Priests: Are you sure the word wasn't "celebrate" in the original Bible instead of the translated "celibate?"

He who breaks wind in church sits in his own pew. (It's in the Bible...somewhere!")

Now they have a "Dial-a-Prayer" for atheists. When you call, nobody answers.

The Lord did not say, "What do you want?"

When I drop my Junior-High aged son off at Sunday School, I like to encourage him to "kick butt!" They have a Foos Ball table in their room for after the class.

One southern Texas preacher remarked that John the Baptist baptized Jesus in the Rio Grande River. (Duh. Everybody knows it was the Mississippi.)

The newspaper did a nice job advertising our "Easter Sunrise Service with breakfast following," except my church didn't have a sunrise service or breakfast planned.

Don't wait for Easter to pray for your keester.

I was the youngest PK in my family for 13 years. One night when Mom was at her nursing job, my oldest brother and I sat down with Dad to play a game. Just before we began, Dad said, in his best Ronald Reagan impersonation, "Well...well...well...your mother is pregnant!" I was elated I would soon have a live doll to play with. My brother's reaction was a bit more cynical and his comment was, "I didn't think you guys did it any more." We have come to accept that our parents are human, even when your parents are the pastor and his wife! So when people ask, "What is it like growing up in a parsonage," I have to chuckle.

One Sunday the church bulletin was typed on pretty pink paper. The pastor announced that he had done this on purpose to remind everyone that Valentine's Day was coming. One man in the congregation muttered that the pink paper reminded him of Pepto Bismal.

The man leading us in prayer used the phrase "blessly riched" instead of "richly blessed."

I was speaking with the new pastor at our church. I wanted to tell him that my son received his masters and bachelors degrees from the University of Illinois. Out of my mouth came, "He received his basters..."

One nun confessed that sometimes she gets silly and makes fun of the Pope.

William Pea was going to say the closing prayer and the song director said, "After we sing this hymn, Brother Pray will Pea for us."

Toward the end of church service, our song director reported that last Sunday's special collection had raised only half the money needed for our new hymnals. He said the church couldn't order them until the full amount was raised, so there was to be another special collection today and each following Sunday until the money was raised. "So," he concluded, "You can either dig deep today or pull the scab off slowly; it doesn't matter, we will raise the money sooner or later." (I guess that's one way of saying it.)

As I stood for a prayer in church I noticed a baseball-sized swelling on the back of my thigh. It was soft, so I wasn't too concerned about it, but I just had to discretely reach down the inside of my slacks to see what it was. I found a rolled-up pair of pantyhose that must have gotten stuck in there from the wash.

My teen-aged son was sitting with some of his friends at church one Sunday. He was misbehaving a bit, so I had this note passed to him in the middle of the sermon. "I took you out for lickings when you were a little guy, I could do it again. Love, Dad."

As a church secretary read the minutes of the last business meeting, she said, "Thirteen members were present and had several erotic discussions. I'm sorry, I mean erratic discussions."

One lady asked if a turkey had had been in the freezer for 23 years was safe to eat. The answer was, "Yes, if it has never been thawed, but the quality would not be good." The lady responded, "That's what I thought. I'll give it to the church."

Next to the church there was a sign pointing to an alternate parking location, with the words "Ample Member Parking." We wondered where members who are not "ample" or do not want to be known as "ample" would park.

In our church bulletin a few years ago was a listing of the craft and other classes being offered after Wednesday night supper. One series, for those who like to sew, was "English smoking" (smocking). I could just see Sir Walter Raleigh and others sign right up.

I went to visit a parishioner in the hospital. I had forgotten what she was being treated for, and as I came into her room, I noticed she was napping. I took her by the toe and wiggled it, saying, "Wake up, sleepy head." She let out a blood curdling scream. Oh, yeah. She had toe surgery. OOPS!

My grandmother has a tendency to drop off to sleep during sermons. She does it enough that there is an unwritten family rule that anyone observing this is to give a gentle nudge to wake her up. This is usually done quickly because Grandma will snore if left in her slumber too long. One Sunday, immediately after her third nudge, Grandma stood up right in the middle of the sermon. She must have been confused in her sleep and thought it was time to go home. It was so funny because only she and the Priest were on their feet. Grandma sat down after a few seconds, but the whole pew was rolling with laughter by then.

My preacher told a hilarious story one Sunday about how we do stupid things sometimes and end up paying the price. He compared it to somebody he did as a child when he and his buddies went out to an empty grain bin. He looked in the doorway and noticed dozens of pigeons roosting inside. He told his friends to watch the pigeons fly when he scared them. He climbed inside the bin and screamed at the top of his lungs, causing a flurry of pigeon activity. He paused in his sermon for a moment and said, "Do you have any idea what a hundred pigeons do when they're scared?"

At a prison church service, one visiting church lady asked the inmates if they ever got congregational visits with their spouses. (Conjugal)

I've got a friend who always takes off his shoes during a sermon…except when I'm sitting behind him, because I'll reach under the pew and take them and not give them back until we're outside.

What we need is to get back to non-skid religion. (Screeeeeeeech!)

They are called the Ten COMMANDMENTS, not Ten SUGGESTIONS!

While dressing after an adult baptism, someone opened the dressing room curtain and exposed the back side of the convert to the congregation.

Used to answering the company phone, the man opened his prayer, "Sawyer Tractor Company," instead of "Dear God."

While praying for the communion, the "fruit of the vine," was referred to as "fruit of the loom."

Asked about what church he attended, the man said, "I belong to the Faith of the Inner Springs Church." (He slept in on Sundays.)

On the way out of a prison service, one well meaning church lady said, "Come and visit us any time," as if they could.

Asked to interpret the Latin words under The Last Supper Picture, he said "All you fellers that want your picture took, get behind the table."

I was listening to a friend reading the selected scripture before the sermon and instead of saying, "The flaming brazier," he said "flaming brassiere."

There was this man who always slept in church. When he was awakened, he would say "Amen," as if he was in silent prayer.

Tennis in the Bible: When Moses served in Pharoah's court.
Baseball in the Bible: In the Big Inning.
The Bible in football: The Immaculate Reception.

The only mention of a car in the Bible: The disciples were in one "accord." (Honda?)

During the spring of each year, given the conditions were right, the sun reflects off a stained glass window and hits our preacher right between the eyes. It's happened enough times that he has become paranoid about springtime.

The song was announced "Amaze me Grace," instead of "Amazing Grace."

On sharing a common communion cup, one gal said, "I believe in God, but I don't think he'll keep me from catching the flu."

Hurrying to church was always a Sunday habit for this family. Finally, settling down, thinking peace had come, their little three-year-old daughter stood up on the seat, grabbed the back of the pew in front of her, and leaned way forward. Low and behold, in their rush to get to church on time, they had forgotten to put panties on her. Half of the audience saw the sweetest little bottom God ever made.

One man's reason for never shoveling the snow, "The Lord giveth, the Lord taketh away."

At a ball game, a fellow church member asked if I knew where the pastor was. I didn't, but my young son jumped in and said, "I just saw him down by the confession stand."

As our adult class was studying about Jonah, my husband said, "I don't think I stomach that."

Not knowing what budget category to put a recent purchase of "Pampers" in, the church secretary finally decided on "Youth Activities."

As I took off my coat in the foyer, I was embarrassed to find myself adorned in the full slip and pull over apron. In my hurry to get everyone ready for church, I had forgotten to dress myself.

One Sunday morning after the sermon, a lady responded to the invitation song and came forward to seek the grace of Jesus. It was customary for the responding member to fill out a card to let the preacher know why she had come, and what she needed in the way of the church.
The preacher noticed this lady looked somewhat puzzled by some aspect of the card, so he went over to help her. He found that he had given her, by mistake, a Christian Camp Enrollment Card. The lady, who had come forward to be baptized, was puzzled by the first question on the form following the name and address: "Can you swim?"

A preacher was telling a parent about his son's swearing and how it interrupted his class. The dad said, "I don't know where that blankety-blank kid gets that stuff!"

I think priests should be allowed to marry. Let them find out what Hell is really like!

I asked a man, "Hey, did you get anything out of my sermon?" He answered, "Yes, a nap!"

An old Indian's estimate of a preacher noted for loud, but useless preaching. "Big wind, great thunder, but no rain."

THE LESSON
Then Jesus took his disciples up the mountain, gathered them around him, and taught them saying:
Blessed are the poor in spirit, for theirs is the kingdom of heaven.
Blessed are the meek, blessed are they that mourn, blessed are the merciful, blessed are they who thirst for justice, blessed are you when you suffer. Be glad and rejoice, for your reward is great in heaven.
Then Simon Peter said, "Do we have to write this down?"
Then James said, "Will this be on the test?"
Phillip said, "I don't have any paper."
Bartholemew said, "Do we have to turn this in?"
And John said, "The other Disciples didn't have to learn this."
And Matthew said, "Can I go to the bathroom?"
And Judas said, "When will we use this in real life?"
Then one of the Pharisees who was present asked to see Jesus's lesson plan and inquired of Jesus, "Where is your anticipatory set of objectives in the cognitive domain?"
...And Jesus wept...

I heard a woman ask the preacher's wife after a Sunday service, "What do you do with him the rest of the week?"

After a sermon, one guy said to me, "That one really put me to sleep."

After driving by the church and seeing a combine in the parking lot, my husband remarked that the Elders must be separating the wheat from the chaff today.

The opening scripture was Psalms 81:10, "Open your mouth wide, and I will fill it." I thought it funny that the man who read it was a local dentist!

Biblical reason for the husband to help around the kitchen: II Kings 21:13, "I will wipe Jerusalem as a man wipeth a dish, wiping it and turning it upside down."

A lady, judging a poster contest at St. Joe Elementary School, thought the only fair way was to go, "Eenie, Meenie, Miney, Mo, catch a Catholic by the toe."

I overheard my doctor husband answer a question from one of our kids, "What's that thing around the pastor's neck?" He said, "That's called a cervical collar." I gently corrected him, "It's referred to as a clerical collar, Dear."

On the outside sign board, the next Sunday's sermon was announced. "We have no wine." By the next Saturday, on top of the board was a bottle of Chablis.

I heard of a church bowling team called the "Holy Rollers."

During a solemn mass, I sneezed and my hat sailed off my head, landing two pews forward. Everyone behind me got a chuckle out of that.

As a young child continued to wail between his two parents, the husband whispered to the wife in measured tones, "WHY DON"T YOU TAKE HIM OUT?" Her soft but deliberate reply was, "I DON"T WANT TO CREATE A SCENE!"

I heard of a time when the choir was walking in an one of the girls got her heel stuck in a heat grate. The boy behind her bent over to pull her heel out but as he lifted the shoe up the entire grate came with it. His momentum carried him forward, and the boy behind him, thinking all was well, took a step forward and ended up in the hole.

I wore a skirt to church that fastened with snaps. We stood as the pastor gave the benediction, and low and behold, my skirt dropped to the floor. It must have come undone while I was sitting and I didn't realize it. No one laughed then, but I'm sure they did on their way home.

I was following a lady out of services one day and watched her walk right out of her slip. Come to find out, the embarrassed lady had forgotten to put her arms through the straps of her slip and so there wasn't anything holding it up.

After singing the closing hymn, a visitor in front of me turning and said on his way out, "Don't give up your day job."

I was observing an adult immersion baptism when I noticed the preacher's underwear showing through his white baptismal clothing after it had become wet. After the service, the preacher's wife was telling everyone that all he had to wear that morning was his Valentine's Day underwear, which happened to have big red hearts all over it!

A sign on the pastor's door said, "Have flu, be back tomorrow, GLW." I finally had to ask the pastor what GLW meant because it wasn't his initials, and he said, "Good Lord willing." I should have known that.

My all-time favorite sermon was titled, "THE LESS YOU SAY, THE LESS YOU HAVE TO TAKE BACK." Good material, and the preacher said it all in 15 minutes.

Bumper Stickers seen in church parking lots:
If you are going the wrong direction, God allows U-turns.

I'd rather be flying.

During the sermon, the preacher made several statements, hoping for some "AMENS." He finally got one when he said "and in conclusion."

Someone at our church got real serious about replacing the pews with 250 recliners.

My arthritis doctor told me he didn't want me on my knees unless I heard the Lord was coming.

A "Sunday only" sign at a car dealer said, "We will not be undersouled."

I got up to the podium to read the selected scripture and said, "Would you please turn to Philations 3:15?" Normally it takes just a few moments for the congregation to thumb to it in their Bible, but for some reason they all just sat there.

I thought maybe they hadn't understood me so I repeated myself, "Philations 3:15". Still, nobody moved. Someone in the front row asked, "Did you mean Philippians or Galations?"

Most got quite a kick out of my "Blooper!"

Our song director, who was also reading the scripture before the sermon said, "Would you please turn your hymnals to Matthew:5."

As I was listening to our pastor speak on the subject of adultery, a helium filled balloon, which escaped from the youth group's party the night before, started settling behind the pastor. The smiley face on the balloon was just a little inappropriate for the sermon topic.

We have a song director that also has a radio show on the local station. One Sunday he said, "The prayer after this song will be brought to you by Jerry Simon…of Simon Auto Sales."

On the marquee in front of the local theater, the movie was advertised, "U FORGIVEN." (with Clint Eastwood) the N and fallen down.

WAYS TO AVOID CHURCH
1. On Saturday night poll your children as to their availability on Sunday morning, then put church attendance to a vote.

2. Plan a late Saturday night with the potential for a good Sunday morning headache.

3. Be sure there is either no gas in the car or the battery is dead.

4. Plan an elaborate Sunday breakfast to ensure that following it there will be no time to dress.

5. At dinner on Saturday discuss those things which bother you about the church and its clergy.

6. In the name of "family togetherness" plan your own three minute Sunday service at home.

7. Make sure that your family is signed up for all Sunday morning "sports opportunities."

8. On Sunday morning "discover" that an important report must be completed before Monday's office arrival.

9. If all else fails, drive your children to church, drop them off, and seek solace in a cup of coffee and The New York Times while you wait for your children go "get religion."

10. Rectors are not supposed to have a sense of humor; boycott those who do.

—*Reverend Walter H. Taylor, Rector. Reprinted with permission—ANGELICAN DIGEST*

NINE COMMANDMENTS FOR ALTAR GUILDS

If it's metal, polish it.

If it's floral, arrange it.

If it's cloth, iron it.

If in doubt, wash it.

If it's been taken care of by one person for more than ten years, avoid it.

If it's a memorial, revere it or try to work around it.

If it's been done only one way for more than five years, don't try to change it.

If new rectors, vicars, or curates get bright ideas, indulge them. They'll soon learn better.

If the bishop wants all the vestments and hanging changed ten minutes before the service, smile sweetly, ask him to pray for a speedy recovery from your hearing loss, and leave him to his prayers in the solitude of the sacristy.

—*via St. Mary's Church, Madisonvilly, KY—Reprinted with permission—ANGELICAN DIGEST.*

EXCUSES WHY PEOPLE DON'T GO TO CHURCH

It's easier to watch what's-his-name on TV.

We went last week.

I knew the pastor in college.

My ex-wife goes there.

My ex-husband goes there.

I haven't sinned much lately.

It makes lunch late.

I can't stand crying babies.

Sitting on pews hurts my hemorrhoids.

The bridge was out.

Turning the song book pages makes my fingers tired.

We didn't want to walk in late, so we didn't go at all.

It exhausts me.

It's none of your business. What are you doing, writing a book?

A local fire inspector, who happened to be Lutheran, walked into a local Church of Christ to do its required inspection. As he wandered around, he walked into a dark room and promptly fell into a filled baptistry.

Now people tease him about getting immersed just in case sprinkling ends up not being scriptural on judgment day.

An elderly gentleman was going to dismiss us with a prayer and he said, "Will you reverently stand on your heads and bow your feet."

FOOTBALL CHRISTIANITY

Quarterback Sneak: Communicants who quietly exit immediately following communion, a quarter of the way through the service or near the last quarter of the service.

Draft Choice: Selection of a seat near the door.

Draw Play: What many children (and a few adults) do with their service leaflets.

Half-time: The time between the peace and the offertory.

Benchwarmer: Those whose only participation is their attendance on Sunday morning.

Fumble: Dropping a hymnal, singing the wrong verse, and general inattention to the prayer book.

Backfield in Motion: Making two or three trips out of the church during the sermon.

Stay in the Pocket: What happens to a lot of money that should go toward missions.

Two-Minute Warning: When the rector begins cleansing the vessels after communion, giving everyone time to shuffle prayer books and hymnals, and gather belongings.

Sudden Death: The rector going overtime.

Blitz: The stampede for the doors after services

Halfback Option: When 50% of the congregation does not return for Evensong.
—*The Angelican Digest, Reprinted with permission 10-28-92.*

While counseling a transient member on job opportunities, I asked him if he had any money. He said he was flat broke. "Not even have $100 tucked away somewhere?" I asked. He said, "If I had $100, I wouldn't need a job."

Out of respect for a dear, 100 year old lady, the congregation sang "Happy Birthday" to her. After everyone applauded, the song director said that we were dismissed. He stopped, looked stupid, and asked one of the Elders if it was scriptural to close a service with the singing of Happy Birthday. Since half the people were already in the aisles, he said it was OK this time.

As I watched a lady hustling across a muddy church yard with her arms loaded down with song books, she caught her heel in the mud and fell flat on her face. Although embarrassed, she stood up, grabbed all the books and started to run up the entry steps. She climbed the steps and as God is my witness, her slacks fell down to her ankles! (Her button & zipper must have come undone when she fell.) I laughed so hard I wet my pants!

Thirty years ago, when my children were very small, Sunday mornings were spent rushing around getting everyone ready. Back then, very high heels were in fashion, so I always waited to put my shoes on until we were nearly ready to leave.

One particular hectic Sunday morning, when we finally collapsed into our church pew, imagine the horror when I looked at my feet and saw my big, fuzzy blue house slippers! I stuck my feet under the pew, wouldn't stand for the prayers, and went out the side exit when church was over.

In the middle of the sermon, an old man belched quite loud. The preacher, engrossed in his speech hadn't heard the belch, only the laughter amongst the congregation. This laughter puzzled him, as he continued.

On his way home, the preacher popped the tape of his sermon into his cassette player, trying to find out what he had said that was so funny. He was relieved when the "belch" came across loud and clear!

When lingering in front of the Catholic church, my cousin was having one last cigarette before attending his first mass. He had never been to church, but I had finally convinced him to go with me.

As services started, I led the way inside the foyer only to turn around and see my cousin douse his cigarette in the holy water receptacle. He said he didn't know whether to throw it away outside or if there was an ash tray inside. When he saw the water, he didn't know any better but thought it very convenient for the church to put one of those things there.

As I walked through the church parking lot, I noticed a van that had a "JESUS" decal stuck directly above the DODGE emblem. It looked like an advertisement for "JESUS DODGE." I had never heard of this dealership, but assumed that if it was legitimate, you would be treated fairly there.

I had a ten-year-old cousin who would stretch out on the pew immediately after the sermon started and fell asleep. I decided to tie his shoes together. As we stood to sing the invitation song, my cousin swung his feet to the floor and stood up. Right after the closing prayer he took one step out into the aisle and fell flat on his face.

As I stood for the benediction, I felt my daughter scrunching behind me on the pew and giving me a big hug. I thought this was sweet of her, until I felt her teeth biting my butt! We went outside for a little chat after that episode.

Before Easter I taught a pre-school class a lesson on the death, burial, and resurrection of Jesus. At one point I said, "Christ arose!"

Four-year-old Johnny went home and told his parents that I said "Christ froze!" It took two more years for him to get that right.

A friend of mine went into the confessional, and instead of saying the customary "Bless me, Father, for I have sinned," she absentmindedly began reciting the common table prayer, "Come, Lord Jesus, be our guest...." The priest fortunately had a terrific sense of humor, because he interrupted her and chuckled, "What'd you do, bring your lunch?"

My little boy was very restless during Mass one Sunday. When communion started, I thought something had finally captured his interest because he calmed down and watched the front of the church intently. He was particularly charmed by the candle with the red globe hanging over the altar. Soon he was fidgeting again and plucked at my sleeve. "Mom, when is that light going to turn green so we can go?" he whispered.

On the way home from a funeral, my five-year-old son asked, "Dad, did the priest really say 'In the name of the Father, Son and in the hole she goes'?"

My four-year-old son was watching the priest walk down the aisle and he said, "Mom, look, there's Hallelujah!"

I was in church one day and toward the end of the service my daughter whispered to me, "Dad, your shirt's inside out."

5

Wedding and Marriage Oops

During my Catholic wedding ceremony, my husband-to-be and I each read biblical passages. The text my husband read (I think it came from 1 or 2 Corinthians) included a reference to having chosen a bride "after zealous investigation." My husband chose me, however, after "zealous indigestion."

The bride suggested to the organist that she play some favorite hymns prior to the processional. Right before the bride was to walk down the aisle, the organist played, "I'd Rather Have Jesus."

An usher at my wedding (who made his living as a waiter) got mixed up while seating one couple, and instead of asking, "Friends of the Bride or Groom," he asked, "Smoking or non-smoking?"

At one wedding the pastor asked the bride if she would "take this man for worse."

At the end of a marriage counseling session, the wife was putting on her coat and she asked her husband if it made her look fat. He said, "No, but your rear end does." I asked her to wait in the car while I had another talk with her husband.

I was at a wedding where the pastor told the groom to "place this fing on her ringer."

I was at a wedding where the pastor said "in the name of the law" instead of "in the name of the Lord."

The pastor at one wedding said, "I now pronounce you man, husband and wife."

As the ringbearer was preceding the bride down the aisle at the wedding, he suddenly stopped, grabbed his crotch, and hollered, "Momma, I gotta pee!"

The wedding was going to be perfect. The planning and worrying were almost over. The groom's car was parked at the church ready for a quick getaway. The time arrived and no groom. First panic, then phone calls. The groom was still at home waiting for his ride to the church. Someone decided the quickest way to get him to the church was to call the police. The groom arrived a bit late in the cruiser, with lights and sirens accompaniment.

While doing a wedding rehearsal for my brother and his fiancé, I came to the part of asking the father "Who gives this daughter away?" I was looking at the fiancé's mother and said "Who gives this mother away?" It woke everyone up, including myself.

While kneeling in front of the pastor, the shoe soles of the groom said,

H   E
L   P

I now "announce" you man and wife.

"Will you take this man to be your wife?"

At this wedding, the seven-year-old ring bearer and the four-year-old flower girl were brother and sister. Before the ceremony started their dad told his son to make sure his sister got down the aisle with the flowers. Big brother ended up dragging her, because she wasn't coming!

One of the bridesmaids got her heel stuck in the heat grate and continued without either shoe on.

I was at a marriage ceremony when the groom fainted and had to be held up by the best man.

During the ceremony, the groom was so emotional that he couldn't recite his vows. The pastor had to change things so he would have to just nod his head, yes or no.

The ceremony was being taped when my husband, the pastor, put the microphone in front of the groom to recite his vows. The groom was so nervous he leaned forward and said "Hello."

The bride fainted during this ceremony and the groom had to carry her out. At least she waited till the end.

The sign on the back of the newlywed's car read, "Just marred."

"Those whom God has joined together, let no one put us under."

Bumper sticker: Don't criticize your wife. If she were perfect, she would have married better.

"I now pronounce you male and female."

My six-year-old son said he was going to be the ring "barrier" at my wedding next month.

After the wedding, we went down to the basement of the church for the reception. There was a big bowl of red punch on the table, and my son said, "Look Mom, they like Bloody Marys just like you do!"

The bride was wearing an old lace gown which fell to the floor as she came down the aisle.

Right after the "I do's" in our wedding ceremony, the old priest unfolded a beautiful white napkin, (I assumed for use in our communion service). He proceeded to honk his nose in it so loud that all in attendance cracked up laughing.

The young pastor, now a Lutheran chaplain in South Dakota, was beaming, as were the bride and groom before him. All had gone well with this, his first wedding. In waiting for the recessional to begin, he leaned over to ask the bride if she wanted to kiss. With that, she leaned over the altar rail, gave the pastor a kiss, then took the groom by the arm and marched out—leaving a very red-faced pastor behind.

At a recent wedding the groom was 15 minutes late. Turning on my portable mike, I headed out to announce to the congregation that the groom had been contacted and that the wedding would take place in another 15 minutes. In the hall I met the custodian and photographer and said couples should pay more attention to wedding times than flowers. This was fine except my mike was on and the congregation overheard the custodian complaining about the lateness of the wedding and his other obligations and so I announced to the congregation, "We should get time and a half for this wedding!" The congregation approved laughingly! Then I proceeded to announce, "I have enough time, I'm going to the bathroom." At the sound of rushing water, one of the parishioners ran down the aisle and yelled into the bathroom and partially over the mike. "Your mike is on!" The most painful part of this experience was having to face all those people with their huge grins when the groom did arrive and the wedding began.

There was a beautiful formal wedding one Sunday afternoon. The minister was a bit hard of hearing. When the time came for the vows to be said, he asked the bride, "Do you take this man..." She answered, "I do."
Silence. The minister instructed her to answer, "I do."
She said, "I did."
"No," said the poor parson, "the answer is, 'I do.'"
Very clearly the bride replied, "I did say I do." By then most of the guests were dissolving in laughter.

6

Contributions from Life, Humor, and Biblican Briefs," the "Lutheran Witness" Magazine, and the "Lutheran" Magazine.

The following excerpts are taken, with the permission from the author, from the book titled, LIFE, HUMOR, and BIBLICAL BRIEFS, by J.A. McNutt.

When I first came to Coleman Avenue church in Memphis, the elders proposed to give me half of the Sunday's contribution as my salary. This was in the midst of the depression and support proved to be pretty small, but as the congregation grew the contributions increased and it was decided by some that the preacher was getting too much money. At my own request, they cut my income by putting me on a regular salary. Later brother W.J. Winn loved to tell that I was the only preacher that he had ever known who preached on commission.

While I was preaching in Arkansas, one Sunday after the morning worship service, the telephone rang, and the lady charged me with making a certain statement in my sermon. I tried to tell her that she evidently misunderstood, and that I had not made the statement. When she insisted that I had done so, my reply was, "Lady, I never believed that in my life, and I am not accustomed to saying things that I don't believe."

In warning men not to think more highly of themselves than they ought to think, I have enjoyed telling the story of the young preacher who had waxed eloquent in his sermon, and had shown an evident lack of humility in reciting his accomplishments. His ego was really deflated by one the elderly sisters, who asked, "Son, has anyone ever told you how wonderful you are?" When he replied, "No sister Jones," she punctured his ego by saying, "How did you find it out?"

Carl Ketcherside was criticizing me continually in his speeches, when finally during a break in the proceedings, I had an opportunity to respond. I told the audience, "Please don't think hard of Carl because of the things he has been saying about me. It reminds me of the case of the little hundred pound woman who was charged with beating her husband, and the judge couldn't understand it because the husband weighed at least two hundred pounds. So he asked the husband, "Why would a big fellow like you let a little woman like this beat up on you?" His reply was, "Well, judge, you see it don't hurt me none, and she gets a lot of pleasure out of it." The audience had a big laugh!

A man on my brother-in-laws farm was a religious man, and the zealous member of the Baptist church. He mentioned that his friend Frank was now a deacon in the Baptist church. When my brother-in-law replied, "I didn't know Frank was a deacon," he replied, "Yes sir, he's done been crowned." I don't know what kind of ceremony was involved, but I have seen a few deacons that needed to be crowned.

One of my favorite stories concerning brother J.D. Tant is about the time he was preaching in a gospel meeting at Coleman Avenue in Memphis, Tennessee, in the early days. It is said that one of our more intellectual and sophisticated preachers was asked to lead the prayer this night, and he used so many words beyond the comprehension of the average audience that brother Tant responded by saying, "John, I hope that the Lord understood what you were saying because I didn't get a word of it."

Someone has said large churches are churches where no one knows anyone else and they are glad they don't, and small churches are churches where everybody knows everybody else and they are sorry they do.

Two surgeons were performing an operation on a patient when a house just outside the hospital operating room caught on fire. As the flames mounted up higher, one doctor said to the other, "John, you had better lower the window shade, our patient may wake up and think that this operation wasn't a success."

Many people are under the impression that the only difference between churches of Christ and Christian Churches is the use or non-use of instrumental music. While in college I had an appointment to preach in a small town, where I had never been before. When I got off the bus near the courthouse, I started out to look for the church building, and meeting one of the local citizens I asked, "Where is the church of Christ?" His reply was in the form of another question, "Fiddlers or non-fiddlers?"

Too many of us are like the Scotsman who said, "God grant that I may always be right, because I never change."

Perhaps you have heard the story of the man at church who, during the sermon, went to sleep and fell off the pew and broke his arm. He went to his lawyer and wanted to sue the church, but the lawyer advised against suing the church saying, "You can't win a suit against the church, but you can sue the preacher for administering an anesthetic without a license."

Perhaps you have heard the story about the old preacher who was involved in a meeting where rainy weather was about to cancel the attendance and he reportedly said, "It is the Lord's meeting, and the Lord's weather, so if he wants to rain out his own meeting, there's nothing I can do about it."

"Every tub should set on its own bottom." That's not in the Bible, but it ought to be.

In one of my early efforts at holding a protracted meeting in a rural area of Mississippi, the services were being interrupted by loud talking outside the building one night. Instead of dealing with the situation in such a way as to provoke more interference, I simply spoke up loud enough to be heard outside and said, "Listen, fellows, we have some brethren who are accustomed to taking a nap during services, and if you don't quit talking so loud you are going to wake them up." Laughter was heard outside and there was no further problem during the meeting.

It is easy to ruin a good bird dog by lending him to strangers. It seems that a fellow had a real first class dog named "Deacon" that was a real good worker in the field trials. He really covered the ground and pointed more birds than some of the best dogs in the country, but some fellows borrowed him for a hunt. They got confused on his name and started calling him "Preacher" and he hasn't done one thing since.

A young man saw a beautiful young lady and was so attracted to her that it was love at first sight. He wanted her for his wife, so he went to his room and began praying to God to help him win her as his bride. However, his prayers were not effective and it seems that God said no to his request.

Fifteen years passed by and then one day he was walking down the street and met the same girl. She was now fifteen years older, and he returned to his room and thanked the Lord for having said "No" to his prayer.

I am told that brother JD Tant was preparing to baptize a fellow in a pond or creek, when the man reached in his hip pocket to retrieve his pocket book and hand it to a friend on the bank. Brother Tant responded by saying, "Put that back in your pocket, I want to baptize it too!" In the course of more than fifty years as a gospel preacher I have observed that we have quite a few "unbaptized pocketbooks" among our brethren.

I heard the story from one of my brethren of an incident that occurred there while brother JD Tant was preaching in a meeting. It seems that while brother Tant was speaking, an old hound dog planted his feet on the front steps of the building and began to howl, whereupon brother Tant ceased to preach and made this request, "Brethren, one of you go out there and kill that dog. He may be called to preach, but this is my appointment."

While preaching at the Second and Walnut Streets church building one Sunday morning, in my enthusiasm I had exceeded the usual time limits for the sermon, much to the dislike of my elderly brethren. Perhaps he had heard the sermon before, and besides he was getting hungry, which provoked his comment. Anyway, the older brother extracted his pocket watch, looked at it closely, put it back in his pocket, and observed to a friend nearby, "Time for dinner ain't it?" I heard the comment up in the pulpit and decided it was time to conclude…How could I have done otherwise?

Perhaps you have heard of the preacher who was troubled by the negative attitude, continued criticism, harassment, and objections of one of the deacons, who closed the worship services with these words, "We will now be led in a few words of criticism by Brother Jones."

Some church members who love to sing, "I'm Standing on the Promises," are merely sitting on the premises.

It has been said that the cooing usually stops when the honeymoon is over, but the billing goes on forever.

Perhaps you have heard of the engaged couple who broke up for religious reasons. It seems that she was a worshipper of money, and he didn't have any.

The new preacher had arrived to work with the church, and the officials were holding a ceremony in which they kept referring to installing the preacher. The little boy sitting next to his father didn't quite understand what was happening so he turned to his father and said, "Do they mean to put him in a stall and feed him?" In reply, the father said, "No, son, they just hitch him to the church and expect him to pull it."

An old brother was having so many problems, and faced trouble he was unable to deal with, so he decided to talk to the Lord about the matter. He left the house and went down to the pasture, knelt down under an old oak tree and began telling the Lord about his troubles. While he was praying, a bird splattered his bald head, and the old fellow arose and said, "See there, Lord, that's what I have been telling you. They sing for some people."

Brother John Gibson of Little Rock, Arkansas, ran this little story in his church bulletin. It seems that some boys were continually crossing a field, and the farmer decided to stop them by erecting a "No Trespassing" sign on his land. This made one of the boys so angry that he vowed that he would get even with the farmer, so he went to the feed store, bought a supply of Johnson grass seed, and sowed every field, fully. Later on he fell in love with the farmer's daughter, and they were married. When the old man died, he inherited the farm and spent the rest of his life fighting Johnson grass. And if you don't understand the situation, you've never lived on a farm.

Shortly after moving to Oklahoma to work with the Central Church in that city, I was officiating a church wedding. My wife came into the auditorium and took a seat in the middle of the building to witness the ceremony. Soon after she was seated, a young lady moved in and sat down beside her and whispered, "How do you like the new preacher?" Whereupon my wife answered softly, "I must like him pretty well, I have been married to him for seventeen years."

THE FOLLOWING ARE BORROWED WITH PERMISSION FROM "THE LUTHERAN WITNESS" MAGAZINE:

Asked by his father how he liked his first day at Vacation Bible School, the four-year-old said, "Just great. We go outside to play, and when we come back in, God has juice and cookies all ready."

While telling the story of the first Christmas, our church's nursery school teacher asked her class, "What did the angel say to Mary?"

No one answered at first, but then little Stephen piped up: "That God was going to be a Daddy soon!"

A pastor asked the youngsters in his children's religion class to define certain churchly terms. Here are the results:

Absolution: Making sure you're right.

Conversion: The point after a touchdown.

Epistle: The wife of an apostle.

False doctrine: Giving someone the wrong medicine.

Hymn: The bottom of a lady's dress.

Redemption: Getting something with green stamps.

A church that prided itself on good fellowship always served coffee after services. One morning, the pastor asked my little daughter if she knew why they served the coffee. "Yes," she said, "It's to help people to get wide awake before driving home."

A little boy was gazing into the crib at his new baby sister, who was lying there crying loudly.

"Did she come from heaven?" the boy asked his mother.

"Yes," the mother said tenderly, "she did."

"Well, with all that noise she's making," he retorted, "it's no wonder they threw her out."

Frustrated because of poor attendance at rehearsals, the choir director called for attention at the last rehearsal before Easter, saying, "I wish to publicly thank the tenor for being the only member of the choir to attend every rehearsal."

"It was the least I could do," the tenor replied, "since I won't be here for Easter."

Our son-in-law is a pastor in the Oklahoma panhandle. Some weeks ago he received a call to another congregation. We were anxious to know whether he would accept it. Finally, his six-year-old called with the news: "Daddy," he announced, "has reclined it."

The kindergarten teacher at our school was reviewing the events of Palm Sunday with her students. She mentioned how even the children waving palm branches sang "Hosanna!"

With this, little Jason spoke up: "I know that one! 'O, Hosanna, oh don't you cry for me!...'"

A father was teaching his young son what a Christian should be like. When the lesson was finished, the father got a spiritual stab that he never forgot: "Daddy," asked the boy, "have I ever seen a Christian?"

My husband, a pastor, keeps a box in his car with tracts, a private communion set, and a small Bible for making visits. On a recent trip, our seven-year-old daughter was paging through the Bible and asked, "Does Problems come before or after Romans?"

After telling the story of Samuel's anointing of young David to be King of Israel, I asked a class of third graders if anyone knew why the old prophet poured oil on David's head.

"Sure," replied one lad, "to make the crown slip on easier!"

The four-year-old boy watched carefully as members of the congregation dropped their offerings into the plate. When the plate approached his father, he whispered, "Don't pay for me, Daddy. Remember, I'm still under five."

Rev. Tom Fast was recently installed as pastor of First Lutheran Church, Natchez, Mississippi. His new circuit counselor is Rev. Rod Loose. Thus, the district now features a couple of pastors who are Fast and Loose.

Our preacher, addressing the congregation, began his sermon thus: "My job this morning, as I understand it, is to talk to you; yours, as I understand it, is to listen. If you finish before I do, just hold up your hand."

The offering was in progress. The two ushers reached each end of the pew in front of us simultaneously, but failed to synchronize their duties. Both started their respective basket down the same pew.

That suggested a collision, but when the baskets reached the center, the graceful young matron, never missing a beat, took one in each hand, crossing one over the other, and continued them on their way.

She did have a trace of a grin on her face, and I'm sure a twinkle in her eyes. So did we in the pew behind her.

When I was a young pastor, an older preacher told me that if I ever forgot the marriage ceremony, I should start quoting scripture until I remembered.

Sure enough, when performing my second wedding, I forgot the words. However, the only scripture I could remember was, "Father, forgive them, for they know not what they do."

Not long ago, our family attended a wedding. The next day, our four-year-old daughter was playing wedding with her dolls. From the next room, I overheard her say, "Do you take this woman to be your awfully lovely wife?"

An announcement about a congregational cookbook recently ran in our church bulletin, "Please submit your favorite recipe," the notice read, "along with a short antidote concerning it."

Little Andy was miffed when he didn't get the part he wanted in the Sunday School Christmas Pageant. He had hoped for the role of Joseph, but got stuck with being the innkeeper instead.

During dress rehearsal, he decided to pull a fast one to get even. So, when Mary and Joseph came to his place seeking shelter, he said, "Sure, folks, come right in. Plenty of room."

The perplexed children playing Mary and Joseph entered and were shown around. But then Joseph, equal to the occasion, said, "Hey, this place is a dump! We'd rather sleep in the stable!"

THE FOLLOWING ARE BORRWED WITH PERMISSION FROM THE "LUTHERAN" MAGAZINE:

This license plate was spotted in Bellevue, Washington: I DODQYR. It belongs to a choir director and stands for: "I do dee choir."

Los Angeles times readers were startled to see the following headline: ST. JOHN PLEADS NO CONTEST TO DRUNK DRIVING until they learned it was a lady's last name and she was given a fine of $1,175 and four years probation.

CHURCH PARKING ONLY—Limited to official church business. Violators' vehicles spirited away at owner's expense.

I overheard a little girl pray, "Lead a snot into temptation, but deliver us from evil."

Seeking to reactivate the church men's group, a few members were trying to think of possible names for the group. Someone said, "How about Men of St. Timothy? Then we could be know as MOST." Someone else responded, "I doubt the ladies will borrow this idea for their group. Then they would be known as LOST."

"NEEDED: Love seat for counseling center."

ENJOY GROUP SINGING?
"INCHOIR" WITHIN!!

Since I work as a university costumer, I was able to help a local congregation to prepare for their re-enactment of the Lord's Supper. On the day after the performance I returned to my shop to find the costumes and a note: "Thanks for all your help." It was signed, "Jesus Christ and the 12 apostles."

Sign in a nursery
"We shall not all sleep, but we shall all be changed."
—1 Corinthians 15:51

I couldn't help but be amused by the sign on the Presbyterian Church: "WATER SHORTAGE? WE SPRINKLE!"

Recently some yard-less friends asked if they could bury their cat in our yard. After they had gone, I insisted my eight-year-old daughter join me in placing a cross on the grave. "Daddy, is that cat a Lutheran?" she asked. "I don't know," I answered. After a few minutes of pondering she responded, "I know, Daddy, it probably was a Catlick!"

Supply houses serving this church are startled when they see that their honorarium checks are signed by the church treasurer, "Robin Hood."

One kid thought the Golden Rule was, "Never let them see you sweat."

A wall plaque in church says, "Never give up." Right next to it at the same eye level is a box in large letters, "OLD HYMNALS."

My six-year-old daughter has her own idea of biblical inerrancy. One day, out of the blue, she asked, "Why doesn't the Bible say, 'By God' on the cover?"

While putting items in my files at Southern Ohio Correctional Facility where I am chaplain, I became aware of two folders in sequence in my drawer. The first is "Death Notices" followed by "Gate Authorizations."

A mother told this story at our adult Sunday School class. She and some friends were discussing the differences between their denomination's beliefs and practices. One woman said, "If you're a Baptist, you always carry your Bible to church." Another said, "The Catholics have to take their rosaries." Then the mother's eight-year-old daughter chimed in, "It's easy being a Lutheran. All we have to bring is our checkbook."

A Baltimore store recently displayed a beautiful Italian-crafted Nativity scene. In the manger where baby Jesus was to be was a small sign that said, "Baby Jesus available upon request." Is there something theological in that?

To keep my younger son quiet in church, I always supply him with a pencil and paper. But I wasn't sure he always paid attention to what was going on during the service. One Sunday the service was especially long with extra hymns and a baptism. After lunch the boys went out into the backyard to play. After a while I heard the sound of water coming from the bathroom. Going to investigate, I saw my son standing by the sink clutching a large grasshopper in one hand and a small bar of soap in the other. He held it under the water and said, "I baptize you in the name of the Father, Son, and the Holy Soap." He HAD been listening in church!

One of our four-year-old members greeted me following our worship service during this year's Olympics. She said, "Hi, pastor. I see the cross that is hanging around your neck is silver. You must be in second place."

Three-year-old Gregory Robinson was costumed as a miniature shepherd for Bethlehem Lutheran Church, Longmont, Colorado's outdoor living Nativity scene. When his mother asked if he'd like to participate next Christmas, Gregory said, "Yes, but next year I'd rather be a pirate."

To give a personal touch to the gift my daughter brought to her Sunday School teacher, I decided to send homemade Christmas cookies. I baked the cookies a few days ahead and put them in one of the empty margarine tubs I use to store food. The Sunday before Christmas I hurriedly took the tub out of the refrigerator and wrapped it in bright Christmas paper. Adding a red bow, I thought it made a pretty present. After church we were all hungry, so my husband offered to get lunch. "There's some tuna left over from yesterday," I told him. After searching the refrigerator for a few minutes, he said, "The only container in here is full of Christmas cookies." To my horror I realized I had given my child's Sunday School teacher the leftover tuna!

My grandmother was a member of Bethlehem Lutheran Church in Fergus Falls, Minnesota. One Christmas Eve their service ended in time for her to attend the last part of the evening celebration at a nearby Lutheran church. Grandma intended to merely watch from the back of the church. But she startled an usher who offered to seat her when she replied, "Oh, no thank you. I just came from Bethlehem."

7

Dear PK

Dear PK,

Sometimes I feel like I've had enough of preaching, counseling, and altogether dealing with church members' problems. I've got problems of my own, don't people know that?

Signed,
Burned out

Dear Out,

Why don't you quit and get a job on the kill floor of a slaughter house and give yourself a little time to figure out what God had in mind for you. Write me back, I care.

Dear PK,

How do I handle the parents of crying babies when they won't take them out during my sermon?

Signed,
They're driving me crazy!

Dear Crazy,

Make anonymous phone calls to these parents in the middle of the night and cry like a baby. They'll get the message.

Dear PK,

My wife keeps falling asleep during my sermons. What should I do?

Signed,
Hurt feelings.

Dear Hurt,

Put her hand in warm water.

Dear PK,

Our P.A. system keeps cutting out during my sermon and the Elders won't get a new one. What should I do?

Signed,

End of my rope.

Dear End,

Next Sunday, just whisper the last half of your sermon. The Elders will think they are losing their hearing and will probably get you a new system...or you'll get fired for being a lousy preacher, but that's the chance you take. This has worked many times before though...good luck.

Dear PK,

There are several people that fall asleep during prayers. How should I handle this problem?

Signed,

Really perplexed.

Dear Really,

Have your congregation stand for all the prayers.

Dear PK,

An old girlfriend has just joined my church. How should I handle this?

Signed,

Dumbfounded.

Dear Dumb,

Simple, act like you don't remember her.

Dear PK,

Contributions are falling off real bad, how can I turn that around?

Signed,

No more money.

Dear More,

Tell your congregation that you will be "called home" if you don't raise a specified amount by a certain date. I heard of a preacher from Tulsa doing this. I don't think it worked for him, but he didn't die either...in case you're worried. Give it a try, what can you lose?

Dear PK,

How do you handle grown-ups who get up in the middle of my sermon to go to the bathroom? Couldn't they go before I started?

Signed,

They're old enough to know better.

Dear Enough,

When these people get up, stop your sermon and ask them to please bring you a glass of water. Shouldn't take over 2-3 times for people to get the message.

Dear PK,

In my adult Sunday school class, there's a man who swears when he gets excited. How do I handle this?

Signed,

Very uncomfortable situation.

Dear Uncomfortable,

Swear right back at him. That'll blow him off his chair. "Oh yeah?" "Yeah!"

Dear PK,

People who come in late interrupt my sermon and cause a general disruption. How can I put a stop to this?

Signed,

It's got to stop!

Dear STOP,

Lock the doors…duh.

Dear PK,

There are several men who show up Sunday morning and look like they have been out all night partying. How can I get them more involved in church activities?

Signed,

Mixed up but good men.

Dear Up,

At the beginning of your next sermon, ask them in front of the entire congregation if they would help out on Saturday nights visiting the elderly and shut-ins.

Dear PK,

Sometimes I feel like I have to do everything at church myself. What should I do?

> Signed,
>
> Not appreciated enough.

Dear NOT,

When it's time to preach your sermon next Sunday, just sit there...that'll get their attention.

Dear PK,

Church members call me at home with church business on Mondays, which is my only day off. How can I get them to stop?

> Signed,
>
> Tired of it.

Dear Tired,

Tell them to meet you at your office in 20 minutes and then don't show up.

Dear PK,

I have a hard time getting people to teach kids' Sunday School classes. What would you do?

> Signed,
>
> Out of gas.

Dear Gas,

Announce that if teachers aren't found, children's Sunday School classes will be held on a rotational basis in members' houses starting next month. That should do it.

Dear PK,

I can't seem to make ends meet on a preacher's salary, what would you do?

> Signed,
>
> Broke

Dear Bro.,

Put on dark sun glasses, act blind and sell pencils on the street corner. I'm sure that will help. God bless, let me know how you do. I care.

Dear PK,

I have a hard time getting the congregation's attention at the beginnings of my sermons. Any advice?

Signed,

About to give up.

Dear Give,

Read them a few pages from this book.

Dear PK,

I run into parishioners everywhere I go. I need some time to myself. What'll I do?

Signed,

In need of privacy.

Dear Need,

Wear Groucho glasses, they'll never know it's you.

Dear PK,

People complain that I'm boring and my sermons are too long. Several of them even fake yawns without covering their mouths.

Signed,

I'm going to walk out.

Dear Out,

...I'm sorry, what were you saying?

Dear PK,

My secretary winked at me during my last sermon. How do I handle this?

Signed,

A little confused,

Dear Confused,

Ask your wife, I'm sure she'll know what to do.

Dear PK,

There are two young couples in my church who act like they are courting during services instead of worshipping. How shall I handle this?

Signed,

Wrong place.

Dear Wrong,

Throw BB's at them.

Dear PK,

There's a guy in my church who always tells "preacher" jokes. I don't like it.

> Signed,
> No more butt of jokes.

Dear Butt,

Lighten up. Any joke he tells about preachers, just tell the same joke in your next sermon but substitute his occupation in the character. He'll love it, I promise.

Dear PK,

Sometimes the associate pastor only preaches 15 minute sermons. What's his problem?

> Signed,
> Feel cheated.

Dear Cheat,

Who cares what his problem is.

Dear PK,

When there's a blizzard, my elders call off church. What can I do?

> Signed,
> Need to worship.

Dear Need,

Put yoooooour HAND on the radio!

Dear PK,

Sometimes I forget to set my alarm clock and end up sleeping through church. I'm sorry, I don't mean to.

> Signed,
> Snoozer.

Dear Snoozer,

Don't worry about it. A lot of people sleep through church…and they'll even there.

Dear PK,

I'm the only one at church who doesn't have a job to do.

> Signed,
> Nobody cares.

Dear Nobody,

So, what's the problem?

Dear PK,

We have a very unruly toddler in our church that disrupts services. What can we do?

> Signed,
> Can't stand it much longer.

Dear Longer,

Have a designated person sit a couple of rows behind this youngster and every time the brat misbehaves, shoot him with a power squirt gun. (From your church supply house.) We MUST teach children how to act in church.

Dear PK,

A grown man keeps breaking wind during church. He should know better. What should I do?

> Signed,
> I've had it.

Dear Had,

Go buy a good bottle of wine, drink it Saturday night and give the tooter the cork on Sunday morning.

Dear PK,

I have a hard time finding a parking spot at church. It makes me so mad I don't even want to go. Any suggestions?

> Signed,
> Running low on gas.

Dear Low,

Don't go. If your church is that packed, nobody will miss you anyway.

Dear PK,

Church is a drag. I should start my own religion.

> Signed,
> Pooped Out.

Dear Pooped,

Go ahead and do it. I'm sure you'll get plenty of support from your present congregation.

Dear PK,

Our church secretary makes numerous mistakes in every Sunday's bulletin. How can I get her to be more careful?

> Signed,
> Tired of it.

Dear Tired,

Don't do anything. Send me the typos if they are funny and tell her to keep up the good work.

Dear PK,

We have an associate pastor who preaches 1 ½ hour sermons. He's great, you don't even notice the time. When can he speak at your church?

> Signed,
> Feel lucky to have him.

Dear Lucky,

When Hell freezes over.

Dear PK,

We have a song director who always pitches the songs wrong. How can I get rid of him?

> Signed,
> My ears hurt.

Dear Ears,

Sing a different song than he' leading. He'll catch on.

Dear PK,
I'm bored.

> Signed,
> Need a hobby.

Dear Hob,
Start a Dear P column.

Dear PK,
There's one man that comes to church who has terrible body odor. Numerous people have had talks with him, but it doesn't seem to do any good. What in the world should we do?

> Signed,
> He really stinks.

Dear Stink,
Write him a letter and say that new members are welcome and anyone joining our church in the next two weeks will be given free rides to church and free dinners following Sunday services.

Sign it with another church's name. (This is probably how he came to be a member of your church anyway.)

8

Associated Hymns

The chiropractor's hymn—*STAND UP, STAND UP.*
The electrician's hymn—*SEND THE LIGHT.*
The poor person's hymn—*I CARE NOT FOR RICHES.*
The rainmaker's hymn—*SHOWERS OF BLESSING.*
The surgical patient's hymn—*I LONG TO BE PERFECTLY WHOLE.*
The day you find out you're pregnant hymn—*O HAPPY DAY.*
The day you find out you're NOT pregnant hymn—*O HAPPY DAY.*
The Mountain Home Builder's Association hymn—*MY HOUSE IS BUILT UPON A ROCK.*
My kid's getting even with me hymn—O THEY TELL ME OF A HOME.
The ranger station hymn—*ON A HILL FAR AWAY*
The physical therapist hymn—*ONE STEP AT A TIME.*
The divorced person's hymn—*OUT OF MY BONDAGE.*
The WIDE LOAD hymn—*PASS ME NOT.*
The rescuer's hymn—*SEEKING THE LOST.*
The fisherman's hymn—*SHALL WE GATHER AT THE RIVER.*
The last payment hymn—*SINCE I CAN READ MY TITLE CLEAR.*
The seamstress hymn—*SOWING IN THE MORNING.*
The dater's hymn—*THE NIGHT IS FAST APPROACHING.*
The thirsty person's hymn—*THERE IS A FOUNTAIN.*
The slingshot hymn—*THERE IS A ROCK.*
The telephone repairman's hymn—*THERE'S A CALL COMES RINGING.*
The dieter's hymn—*THOU, MY EVER LASTING PORTION.*
The hiker's hymn—*WALKING IN THE SUNLIGHT.*
The chain gang hymn—*GO LABOR ON.*
The car accident hymn—*WE SAW THEE NOT.*
The lawyer's hymn—*WHEN ALL MY LABORS AND TRIALS ARE O'ER.*
The street crossing guard hymn—*WHY DO YOU WAIT?*

The prisoner's hymn—*WOULD YOU BE FREE.*
The home builder's hymn—*A MIGHTY FORTRESS.*
The parade master's hymn—*FLING OUT THE BANNER.*
The weatherman's hymn—*FROM EVERY STORMY WIND THAT BLOWS.*
The Darning Association's hymn—*HOLY, HOLY, HOLY.*
The Girdle Association hymn—*HOW FIRM A FOUNDATION.*
The caterer's hymn—*ALL THINGS ARE READY, COME TO THE FEAST.*
The salesman's hymn—*ALMOST PERSUADED.*
The insurance man's hymn—*BLESSED ASSURANCE.*
The cowboy's hymn—*DAY IS DYING IN THE WEST.*
The accountant's hymn—*EARTH HOLDS NO TREASURES.*
The traveler's hymn—FAR AND NEAR.
The scuba diver's hymn—*FAR AWAY IN THE DEPTHS.*
The whisperer's hymn—*HARK! THE GENTLE VOICE.*
The whining spouse hymn—*HAVE THINE OWN WAY.*
The wagon master's hymn—*HE LEADETH ME.*
The hearing aid salesman's hymn—*HEAR THE SWEET VOICE.*
The lost traveler's hymn—*HERE WE ARE BUT STRAYING PILGRIMS.*
The oxen hymn—*HIS YOKE IS EASY.*
The new kid in class hymn—*I AM A STRANGER HERE.*
The rookie hang glider's hymn—*I AM DWELLING ON THE MOUN-TAIN.*
The Vegetable Grower's Association hymn—*I COME TO THE GARDEN ALONE.*
The explorer's hymn—*I HAVE HEARD OF A LAND.*
The watch repairman's hymn—*I NEED THEE EVERY HOUR.*
The Job Service hymn—*I WANT TO BE A WORKER.*
The ironing lady's hymn—*I'M PRESSING ON.*
The distiller's hymn—*I REACHED THE LAND OF CORN AND WINE.*
The lost dog hymn—*I'VE WANDERED FAR.*
The half time Alaska hymn—*IN THE LAND OF FADELESS DAY.*
The birthday hymn—*IS IT FOR ME?*
The night watchman's hymn—*IT MAY BE AT MORN.*
The nervous groom's hymn—*JUST A FEW MORE DAYS.*
The perfect person's hymn—*JUST AS I AM.*
The drunkard's hymn—*LEAD ME GENTLY HOME.*

The psychiatrist hymn—*LET US WITH A GLADSOME MIND.*
The pie maker's hymn—*PEACE, PERFECT PEACE.*
The Gold Collector's Association hymn—*PURER YET AND PURER.*
The Rock Collector's Association hymn—*ROCK OF AGES.*
The dynamite specialist hymn—*SAFELY THROUGH ANOTHER WEEK.*
The race car hymn—*SPEED AWAY.*
The payment book hymn—*WE GIVE THEE BUT THINE OWN.*
The escaped convict's hymn—*FLEE AS A BIRD.*
The coal miner's hymn—*SOMEWHERE THE SUN IS SHINING.*

I have with reluctance, deleted many stories that relate to body parts, body functions and/or have questionable overtones. Some people feel such stories, although true, contaminate. That could hinder Christian book stores from stocking it and I want THE BIG BOOK OF CHURCH HUMOR in every book store in the English speaking world.

Copies of these hurtled stories can be had by sending $5 (cash or check) and a self-addressed-stamped business envelope to:

Ken Alley
PO Box 397
York, Ne. 68467

BOOK 2

Heavenly Hoots

Whatever trouble Adam had
No man in days of yore
Could say when he had told a joke,
"I've heard that one before."

—Anon

Contents

1

Your Halo's Askew (Preachers)

Good introduction—A visiting preacher agreed to fill the pulpit of an ill preacher one Sunday. The elder introducing the speaker said, "This noted clergyman is one of the greatest men of the age. He knows the unknowable, he can undo the undoable, and he can unscrew the unscrutable!"

Thunder and lightning—A bishop came to visit a church to hear the minister preach. The pastor spoke loudly and with many sweeping hand gestures. When he finished the service, he approached the bishop and asked how he liked the sermon.

The bishop answered, "Pretty well, but don't you think you spoke a little loud?"

"Well, it's this way," said the preacher, "what I lack in lightning I try to make up in thunder."

The parson's duty—Dull sermons mean lazy preachers. The preacher halted in his sermon one Sunday morning and said, "Brother Simmons, wake that man next to you, please."

"Wake him up yourself," said Simmons, "you put him to sleep."

His hobby—A minister was very fond of preaching on the subject of water baptism. On one occasion his official board asked him to preach from a certain text which they selected, thinking it would be impossible for him to bring in water baptism. They chose for his text Genesis 3:9—"And the Lord God called unto Adam and said unto him, 'Where art Thou?'" The minister accepted the text and on Sunday morning announced, "I will divide my text into three parts: First, where Adam was; second, where Adam should have been; and third, a few scattering remarks on water baptism."

All the prones—PARSON (in fervent prayer): "Oh, Lord, this little congregation of mine is prone to gossip! Oh, Lord, this little congregation of mine is prone to steal! Oh, Lord, this little congregation of mine is prone to do things that are wrong in the house of the Lord! O Lord! Deliver us from the prone."

Passing sighs—The pastor was fond of using figures of speech. At a funeral he began his address, "Friends, we have here only the shell of the man. The nut is gone."

Gentle preaching to rich sinners—A bishop is said to have described the preaching of some ministers to aristocratic members as follows: "Brethren, you must repent, as it were, and be converted, in a measure, or you will be damned to some extent."

Scattering remarks—A farmer's boy was sent to a large woodland pasture to bring home the cows, but returned after an hour's absence without the cows.
"Why didn't you bring the cows, son?" asked the father.
"Couldn't find 'em," was the reply.
"That's strange. Where did you look for them?"
"Oh, I just looked everywhere."
"Well, tell me where you went," sternly demanded the father.
"I first went up there to the end of the lane," said the boy, "then I just scattered."
Some preachers discuss a subject in about the same manner.

Brevity please—Long, drawn-out introductions are usually a bore. The old retired pastor had the right idea. He was called upon to introduce a guest speaker on Sunday. When it came time for the sermon, he said, "My friends, I have been asked to introduce Pastor Jameson who is to preach to you. Well, I have done so and he will now do so."

Practicing what you preach—"Then you don't think I practice what I preach, eh?" the minister asked one of his deacons at a meeting.
"No, sir, I don't," replied the deacon. "You've been preaching on the subject of resignation for two years, and you haven't resigned yet."

Superlative—The little church was celebrating its 100th anniversary and the pastor introduced the guest speaker enthusiastically, "Brothers and sisters, this church has had the privilege of hearing some of the highest ranking preachers in the state. But today, my friends, we have the honor of hearing the rankest preacher we have ever had in the pulpit!"

Thwarting the devil—The preacher of a small congregation called upon the preacher of a very large congregation and found him busy writing.

"What are you doing?" the first preacher asked.

"I'm preparing notes for my sermon next Sunday," replied the second.

The first preacher shook his head. "I certainly would never do that," he said. "The devil is looking right over your shoulder and knows everything you're going to say and he is prepared for you. Now, I don't make any notes, and when I get up to talk, neither I nor the devil know what I'm going to say."

Wake up the preacher—When somebody asked Brother Beecher what he did when the members of his congregation began to yawn, he said that the janitor has explicit orders under those circumstances to walk up the aisle of the church and wake up the preacher.

Apology—A preacher who had had a very hectic week found himself Sunday morning with no sermon prepared. He spoke frankly before his congregation. "Beloved," he said, "I deeply regret that it has been impossible for me to prepare a sermon. I can do no better than open my mouth and let the Lord speak through me. Next Sunday I hope to do better."

Something to approve—"Was the sermon to your liking, Patricia?" asked the preacher.

"It was simply grand," gushed the woman. "I especially admired your perseverance—the way you went over the same thing again and again and again."

Difficult to locate—An old preacher was standing by the grave of a departed parishioner, who had gaily pursued worldly pleasures all his life. Sorrowfully gazing at the ground, the pastor spoke, "Farewell, brother. We hope you've gone where we think you aren't!"

His failing—A minister whose style was to use big words and complicated discourse was called to a church committee meeting. There he was told his manner of preaching was lacking.

Dumbstruck, the minister asked, "Don't I argify and sputify?"

"Yes, you argify and sputify," responded a member of the committee, "but you don't show wherein."

The silent method—When the term of the old preacher expired, he arose and said, "Brothers, the time is here for the election of your pastor for another year. All those favoring me for your pastor will please say, 'Aye.'" The old preacher was rather unpopular, so there was no response. "Ha," he said, "silence always gives consent. I'm your pastor for another year."

Sign of something—"Do you think they approved of my sermon?" asked the newly appointed rector, hopeful that he had made a good impression.

"Yes, I think so," replied his wife, "they were all nodding."

Circular oratory—"Gentlemen," began the speaker, "my opinion is that the generality of mankind in general is disposed to take advantage of the generality of—"

"Sit down, son," interrupted an old man in the audience, "you're coming out of the same hole you went in."

Poor stuff—A new minister in a rural district met an old farmer in his congregation. Stopping the man on the street, the minister asked, "Mr. Brown, how did you like my sermon last Sunday?"

"Well, parson," replied the old man, "you see, I didn't have a fair chance to judge. Right in front of me was old widow Smith and the others widows in her group, with their mouths wide open just a swallowing down all the best of your sermon. What reached me, Parson, was pretty poor stuff indeed."

There they go—A minister preached a rather long sermon from the text, "Thou art weighed in the balance and found wanting." After the congregation had listened for some time a few began to grow weary and went out. Others soon followed, to the annoyance of the minister. Whereupon he stopped his sermon and said, "That's right, gentlemen, as fast as you are weighed, pass out."

Our sufficiency in God—A Puritan preacher, asking a blessing on a meal consisting of a herring and potatoes, said, "Lord, we thank Thee that Thou hast ransacked sea and land to find food for Thy children."

Accuracy in prayer—A story is told of a minister who was a great precisionist in the use of words, his exactness sometimes destroying the force of what he was saying. On one occasion in the course of an eloquent prayer, he pleaded, "Oh, Lord, awaken Thy cause in the hearts of this congregation. Give them new eyes to see and new impulses to do. Send down Thy lev-er or lee-ver according to Webster's of Worcester's dictionary, whichever Thou usest, and pry them into activity."

Serve them right—Minister's wife: "Wake up! There are burglars in the house!"

Minister: "Well, let them find out their mistake themselves."

Misrepresented—After the marriage ceremony the minister shook hands with the groom and remarked that now his troubles were at an end. The young man came back to the preacher a month later and said, "You misrepresented things when you told me that my troubles were at an end."

"I told you the truth," replied the minister, "but I didn't tell you which end—I meant the beginning end."

Strictly business—A clergyman continually pestered his bishop with appeals for help and it soon became necessary to tell him that he must not send any more appeals. His next communication was as follows: "This is not an appeal. It is a report. I have no pants."

Never let go—A preacher, when asked to define "perseverance," said, "It means firstly, to take hold; secondly, to hold on; and lastly, to never let go."

Paying for what they got—The pastor had served the congregation the entire year and received only five thousand dollars for his service. A friend said to him, "Five thousand dollars for a year's preaching isn't very much, is it?"

"No," replied the preacher, "but you should have heard the preaching they got."

Keeping them in—Mr. Manning once preached in a church where members of the congregation had the habit of leaving before the close of the service. Warned of this beforehand, Preacher Manning opened the sermon by saying encouragingly, "I am going to speak to two classes today; first, the sinners, and then to the saints." After earnestly addressing the supposed sinners for awhile, he said that they could now take their coats and go. The entire congregation heard him to the end.

Important announcement—A pastor startled his congregation by the announcement, "Remember our quarterly meeting next Sunday. The Lord will be with us during the morning service, and the presiding elder in the evening."

Experience the better teacher—The archbishop had preached a fine sermon on married life and its duties. Two elderly women walked out of church together commenting on the address. "That was a fine sermon his Reverence gave us," said one to the other. "It was indeed," was the quick reply, "and I wish I knew as little about the matter as he does."

Wandered—The old preacher officiated at the college chapel; and although his sermon was excellent in itself, it had no obvious connection to the text. At dinner the young preacher was asked his opinion of the sermon.

"Why, it was truly apostolic! He took a text, and then went everywhere preaching the gospel."

A center shot—A member of the congregation, becoming angry at a sermon the minister was preaching, wrote a single word, "Fool," on a sheet of paper, called an usher to him and had it delivered to the minister in the middle of his sermon. The minister opened the paper and read what was written, then he said, "An unusual thing has happened. A member of the congregation has signed his name without writing the letter."

Religious economy—A rabbi worked for a small stipend and was asked by a friend how he was getting along. "Slowly," he answered with a sigh. "If it were not for the numerous fasts which our religion prescribes, I'm sure my family would die of starvation."

A gentle hint—A visiting preacher asked an usher how long he should speak. The usher replied, "There's no limit on the length of your sermon, sir, but I will suggest that the most souls are saved during the first twenty minutes."

Running the gauntlet—Usually the minister during his first year is idolized, the second, criticized, and the third, ostracized.

They wish he would—A truly eloquent parson had been preaching for nearly an hour on the immortality of the soul. "I look at the mountains," he declared, "and cannot help thinking, 'Beautiful as you are, you will be destroyed, while my soul will not.' I gaze upon the ocean and cry, 'Mighty as you are, you will eventually dry up, but not I.'"

A good substitute—A minister had been away on a vacation, and on his return asked the sexton how all had gone in his absence. "Very well," was the response. "I hear that most ministers leave someone worse than themselves to fill the pulpit when they go away, but you never do that, sir."

Appraising the minister—The man was asked what he thought of his new minister and replied, "I don't think much of him, really. Six days he's invisible and the seventh he's incomprehensible."

Unfortunate introduction—A pastor introducing a visiting minister said, "I take pleasure in introducing to you Pastor Gordan, who will address us on the subject of 'The Devil.' I can assure you the pastor is full of his subject."

The unkindest cut—A minister came before his Sunday morning congregation with one of his fingers bandaged. After the service a man asked him what had happened to his finger.

"I was shaving this morning," said the minister, "had my mind on my sermon and accidentally cut my finger."

"That's too bad," replied the sympathetic man. "However, I hope the next time you will have your mind on your finger and cut your sermon."

The gospel is enough—A young man wanted to preach. He went to school to prepare himself for the ministry, but decided to quit after a few months and go right to preaching. His friends and teachers argued to him that he should continue his studies and thoroughly prepare himself for the ministry.

"I don't see any need of continuing any longer in school," he said. "All I mean to preach is just the gospel."

Good use for them—The minister answered the doorbell. "I'm collecting for the poor," said the caller. "Do you happen to have any old clothes?"

"Yes," answered the minister.

"Would you be willing to give them to me? I can assure you they will be put to good use."

"No, I cannot give them to you."

"Why not? What do you do with them?"

"Each night I brush them carefully, fold them, and hang them over a chair. In the morning I put them on again."

Low salaries—An elderly bishop always advocated paying better salaries to ministers. He told of a capable young fellow, hopeful and happy in his pastorate in spite of the low pay. He lost touch with him for several years, when suddenly he met the young man in Boston, looking prosperous. "What church are you in now?" asked the bishop.

"No church," the man said regretfully, "I'm now in the banking business."

"Why did you leave the church?" asked the bishop.

"For seven reasons."

"What are they?"

"A wife and six children."

Simple enough—The preacher was recovering from an illness and was refusing all visitors. There was one man in the congregation who was wealthy, but miserly toward the church and everyone else. When he called on the pastor, he was received at once.

"I appreciate this very much," said the man, "but why do you see me when you refuse to see your friends?"

"I feel confident of seeing my friends in the next world," replied the preacher, "but I feel this may be my last chance of seeing you."

More exact—At a meeting of he church board the minister announced that he had a call to another parish. After wishing him well in his new parish, one of the deacons asked how much more salary he was going to get.

"Three hundred dollars," the minister replied.

"I don't blame you for going. But, Parson, don't you think you should be a bit more exact in your language? That isn't a 'call,' that's a 'raise.'"

Plenty of time—The minister of a parish in a small village was walking home one foggy night when he fell into a deep hole. There was no foothold to help him get out, so he began to shout for help. A passing drunk heard his cries and asked the man who he was. When the minister told him, the drunk replied, "I'll be on my way then. You're not needed until Sunday and this is only Wednesday night."

The widow's spite—"Mrs. Smithers seems very cross with me," the pastor remarked to a friend. "Did you notice how she snubbed me?"

"I'm not surprised," replied the friend. "Don't you remember when you preached her husband's funeral? In the sermon you said, 'He has gone to a far better home.'"

Sad answer—A clergyman accepted an invitation to officiate at Sunday services in a neighboring town, and told his new curate to give the sermon at his home church. On returning home, the preacher asked his wife what she thought of the curate's sermon.

"It was the poorest one I ever heard," she replied promptly, "nothing in it at all."

Later in the day the clergyman asked his curate how he had gotten along. "Oh, very well," was the reply. "I didn't have time to prepare anything, so I preached one of your unused sermons."

Taking precautions—A young and nervous minister was asked if he thought it was wrong to take a walk in the country on Sunday afternoons. "Well," he responded cautiously, "I suppose there is really no harm taking a bit of a walk on the Sabbath, so long as you don't enjoy yourself."

Handicapped—A preacher timidly began his address by saying, "I have not had very much experience in public speaking. For a number of years I sang in a quartet and the director of the quartet did about all the speaking. Shortly after I left the quartet I got married, and I haven't had the chance to get in very many words since."

The pessimistic pastor—The very young clergyman made his first parochial call. He tried to admire the baby and asked how old it was. "Just ten weeks," the proud mother replied.

The young minister inquired interestedly, "And is it your youngest?"

The Lord needed help—A preacher was giving his sermon one Sunday when fire engines raced past the church, breaking the attention of the congregation. "Sit still!" the preacher commanded. "If there is a fire the Lord will take care of his own and not let anything happen that shouldn't."

Just then two children, who had stepped outside, shrieked, "It's the parsonage!" Without a word, the preacher made a wild dash from the pulpit and streaked to his burning residence.

"It seems there are times when the Lord needs help," said a wise member of the congregation.

Faith rather than hearing—An inexperienced minister was called upon to speak at a gathering. He was very nervous, but determined to do his duty. He took the podium reluctantly and began, "I am not much of a speaker yet, friends."

"Amen!" came heartily from a member of the audience.

The preacher was troubled, but manfully proceeded, "I shall detain you for just a moment."

"Hallelujah!" came from the same member.

The preacher proceeded to make a few remarks, although much embarrassed. He laughed heartily, however, when it was explained to him that the exclamations had come from a deaf man who was able to recognize nothing but the pauses in his speech, and had expressed his approval on faith rather than hearing.

He quite agreed—In the old days, a minister had a servant who was smart and ambitious, but was unable to read or write. One Sunday the minister saw his servant in church, scribbling away frantically through the sermon. Afterward the minister asked him, "Timothy, what were you doing in church?"

"Taking notes, sir, I'm eager to learn."

"Let me see," said the minister, and he glanced over Timothy's notes, which looked more like chicken scratches than words. "Why, Timothy," he said gently, "this is all nonsense."

Timothy nodded his head, "I thought so too, all the time you were preaching it."

Large order—"And what is the baby's name?" asked the pastor softly.

The father smiled proudly as he hoisted the little fellow up in his arms, "Charles William Robert Montgomery Finley."

The pastor's eyebrows shot up as he turned to his assistant, "More water, please."

He knows your measure—A wealthy widow went to hear a well-known traveling preacher. She noticed that his clothes were somewhat worn and shabby. At the close of the service she told the preacher that she would be happy to give him some of her deceased husband's clothes, if they would happen to fit him.

"Did the Lord tell you to give them to me?" asked the preacher.

"I believe he did," was the reply.

"Well, then, if the Lord told you to give them to me you need not fear about their fitting me. The Lord knows my measure."

Opposition overcome—Only one of the elders opposed the new candidate becoming the pastor of their church. The pastor asked the man why he was against his becoming their new pastor.

"I like your personality," was the reply, "but I don't like your sermons."

"Then we agree," replied the candidate. "I don't like my sermons very well myself, but how foolish it would be for you and me to set our opinions against that of the whole parish!"

The humor of this reasoning appealed to the man and he withdrew his objection.

Love wanting—One preacher was thoroughly disgusted with his congregation and had found his calling in another town. For his last sermon he gave his reasons for leaving: "First, you do not love me, for you have contributed nothing to my support. Second, you do not love each other, for I have not celebrated a marriage since I arrived. Third, the good God does not love you, for he has not taken one of you to himself. I have not had a single funeral."

Plenty left over—A young pastor announced nervously one morning, "I will take for my text the words, 'And they fed five people with five thousand loaves of bread and two thousand fishes.'" At this misquotation an old man in the congregation said audibly, "That's no miracle; I can do it myself."

The young preacher said nothing at the time, but the next Sunday he announced the same text. This time he got it right, "And they fed five thousand people on five loaves of bread and two fishes." He waited for a moment, then leaned over the pulpit and looked at the old man, saying, "Could you do that too, Mr. Smith?"

"Of course I could," Mr. Smith replied.

"How would you do it?" asked the preacher

"Why, with what was left over from last Sunday, of course."

The report confirmed—An old woman was sick one Sunday and was unable to attend church. The pastor visited her during the week and she explained to him why she had not been present.

"I suppose you didn't miss much," said the pastor jokingly.

"That's what I hear," she answered.

Not the trout's fault—A minister settled near the headwaters of a fertile river. He was a good man, full of humor and quick wit. One Monday morning a parishioner presented the minister with a string of fine trout. The minister thanked him solemnly for the gift.

"But, Pastor," smiled the parishioner, "those fish were caught yesterday. Perhaps your conscience won't let you eat them."

"John," replied the minister, "there's one thing I know. The trout were not to blame."

Warning—When the minister noticed some of his elders sleeping during the sermon, he suddenly shouted loudly, "Fire, fire!"

The elders awakened, alarmed, and cried out, "Where, sir, where?"

"In hell!" they were told firmly. "In hell for those who sleep during the preaching of the word."

Cause enough—A divinity student named Tweedle
Once wouldn't accept his degree.
'Cause it's tough enough being called Tweedle
Without being Tweedle D.D.

Making it clear—A preacher used the word "phenomenon" in his sermon. At the close of the service, one of his congregation asked the meaning of the word. The preacher replied, "If you see a cow, that's not a phenomenon. If you see a thistle, that's not a phenomenon. And if you see a bird that sings, that's not a phenomenon. But if you see a cow sitting on a thistle and singing like a bird, then that's a phenomenon."

Anticipating the worst—The minister who made the following announcement seems to have been prepared for negative results from his preaching, "There are some flowers here for those who are sick at the close of service."

How true—A bishop of the Methodist Church, when asked to name the two books which had most influenced his life, replied, "My father's checkbook and my mother's cookbook."

Told the truth—The minister intended to preach from 1 Corinthians 13:1. He asked the church secretary to type up the text for him so it would be easier to read. She accidentally typed an "l" instead of an "h," so the minister read the following words, "Though I may speak with the tongues of men and of angels if I have not clarity I would only be sounding as brass or tinkling cymbal."

Unwelcome caller—The handsome young minister always greeted his parishioners as they filed out. One Sunday morning along came a young woman, a new member of the church. With his usual cordiality, the minister grasped her hand and said, "I am glad to see you here this morning. Will you give me your name and address so I may call on you soon?" The girl looked at him coldly, withdrew her hand and replied, "I thank you, but I've got a steady fellow, and I think he wouldn't like you to come."

Sharp point too—The sexton had been laying the new carpet on the pulpit floor and had left a number of tacks scattered about.

"See here, James," said the parson, "what would happen if I stepped on one of those tacks right in the middle of my sermon?"

"I guess there'd be one point you wouldn't linger on," replied the smiling sexton.

Gross darkness—The pastor was preaching, "'The darkness shall cover the earth, and gross darkness the people.'" He continued, "There may be some of you who don't know what gross darkness means. Well, it's just exactly 144 times darker than dark."

Long sermons—The minister was rather long-winded, and late in the sermon a young wife of the congregation remembered that she'd left the Sunday dinner in the oven without turning down the heat. She hastily wrote a note and slipped it to her husband, who was an usher. He thought it was for the minister and calmly walked up and laid it on the pulpit. The minister paused, read the note, then frowned at the message, "Shut off the gas."

Great damage, apparently—A student was sent one Sunday to fill in at a vacant pulpit in a small valley town. A few days afterward he received a copy of the village paper from the little town, with the following item marked: "Rev. Thomas of the senior class at Seminary supplied the pulpit at the Congregational church last Sunday, and the church will now be closed three weeks for repairs."

Long known—"Father," said the minister's son, "my teacher says that 'collect' and 'congregate' mean the same thing. Do they?"

"Perhaps they do, son, but you may tell your teacher that there is a vast difference between a congregation and a collection."

The truth—After he had been with his congregation a short time, the minister struck up a friendship with a prominent citizen. One day the man told the preacher, "Pastor, you are certainly the best preacher who has ever been here."

"Well, James," replied the minister modestly, "there must have been some sorry ones here then."

The man replied cheerfully, "Yes, sir, that's the truth!"

The useless preacher—A young boy was crying very bitterly because his wagon was broken. A kind-hearted passerby tried to cheer up the little fellow by saying, "Never mind, my boy, your father can easily fix that."

"No, he can't," sobbed the boy. "My father is a preacher and doesn't know about anything!"

Dry-cleaned—The Baptist preacher had just finished an enthusiastic exhortation. "Now, brothers and sisters, come up to the altar and have your sins washed away."

All came but one. "Brother Washington, don't you want your sins washed away?"

"I've already had my sins washed away."

"You have! Where'd you get it done?"

"Over at the Methodist church."

"Ah, Brother Washington, you haven't been washed, you've just been dry-cleaned."

It took quick thinking—A preacher had at one time served a short jail sentence and was fearful that his congregation would one day discover this fact. One Sunday, rising to begin his sermon, his heart sank to see his former cellmate sitting in the front row. Thinking quickly, he fixed his eye on the unwelcome guest and announced solemnly, "I take my text this morning from Job 64, which says, 'He who sees and knows me and says nothing, him will I see later.'"

Dive deep but come up soon—Church service was over and three prominent members walked home together, discussing the sermon. "I tell you," said the first enthusiastically, "Pastor can certainly dive deeper into the truth than any preacher I ever heard."

"Yes," said the second man, "and he can stay under longer."

Added the third, "And come up drier."

Leave financial matters to others—The minister was ignorant of financial matters. He once received a check—the first one he ever saw in his life—and took it to a bank for payment. "You must first endorse the check," said the teller, returning it through the little window. "It must be endorsed on the back."

"I see," said the minister. And turning the check over he wrote across the back of it, "I heartily endorse this check."

Secure a heavenly minister—A country church offered such a very small salary that the applicant wrote the trustees: "The only individual I know who could exist on such a stipend is the angel Gabriel. He would neither need cash nor clothes and would come down from heaven every Sunday morning and go back at night. So I advise that you invite him."

What were you saying?—CLERGYMAN: "I brought back the used car I bought from you last week. It's too temperamental."

DEALER: "What's wrong? Can't you run it?"

CLERGYMAN: "Not and stay in the ministry."

Danger in borrowed outlines—An evangelist dropped in to hear a pastor friend preach. The sermon so impressed him that he asked to borrow the outline for his use. This was gladly granted.

One Sunday morning after preaching this borrowed sermon, a visitor said to him, "I certainly enjoyed your sermon this morning. It was the best I've ever heard preached from that text. Our pastor preached from that text some time ago, and although he didn't get as much out of it as you did, I certainly think he must have gotten his outline from you."

Preaching or talking—The evangelist had preached for several evenings, exposing the shortcomings and inconsistencies of the members of the church in blunt terms. His manner of preaching stirred up the wrath of some prominent members, and grumblings were heard on every hand. One complainer went to the janitor and asked him if he meant to build fires and keep the house in order for such a preacher as this evangelist. The old janitor replied, "Oh, I don't pay attention to him when he talks, I only listen when he preaches."

Asking largely—The new minister in church was delivering his first sermon. The old janitor was listening critically from the back corner of the church. The minister's sermon was flowery and his prayers seemed to cover the whole category of human wants. After the service one of the elders asked the janitor what he thought of the new minister's prayers.

The old gent replied, "Why, that man asked the good Lord for things that our other preacher didn't even know we needed!"

Christians are watched—The minister was nailing shingles on his roof when a small boy stopped and watched for some time. "Well, young man," he said pleasantly, "are you interested in carpentry?"

"No," said the boy, "I was waiting to see what a preacher will say when he hammers his thumb."

And still at it—A man was fined by a magistrate for sleeping and snoring in church. Nothing was done to the clergyman for putting him to sleep.

The long and short of it—A popular preacher once stated, "A sermon should be like a woman's dress—long enough to cover the subject, but short enough to be interesting."

The fundamentals—A little boy, who had a stuttering problem, was once asked by a visiting bishop if he would like to be a preacher.

"I w-w-would l-like to d-d-do the p-pounding and the h-hollering," he replied, "but the s-speaking w-w-would b-bother me s-some."

Speaking difficulties—The preacher was having a hard time getting his message across. One by one the audience got up and left. This continued for some time and finally the preacher paused and said, "I don't blame you for leaving. I would go too, but I've got to stay here and preach."

A lady was very upset when she learned that her pastor would not return to her church for the next year. The dear pastor tried to comfort her with the assurance that the synod would send her a good pastor for the next year.

"I don't know about that," she said, "it seems to me that each time we have a change they get poorer and poorer."

A minister was deeply impressed by an address on the evils of smoking given at a recent seminar. He rose from his seat, went over to a fellow minister and said, "Brother, this morning I received a gift of 100 good cigars. I've smoked one of them, but now I'm going home to burn the remainder in the fire."

The other minister rose and said he would come along. "I intend to rescue the ninety and nine," he added.

"What an inspiring sermon your husband preached on 'One Day's Rest in Seven!'" stated the visitor.

"I didn't hear it—I had to get his dinner," replied the pastor's wife.

One Sunday morning the pastor woke up feeling quite queasy. He called his servant and said, "Jeffery, I want you to go to my assistant and tell him that he'll have to officiate for me this morning."

Jeffery thought for a moment, then talked to his master and finally persuaded him that he would feel better if he officiated as usual. The minister was surprised to find that he did, indeed feel better after services.

"You're better?" asked the servant, meeting his master at the door.

"Very much, thank you, Jeffery."

The servant grinned. "What did I tell you! I knew you'd be alright just as soon as you got that sermon out of your system."

The sermon was dry and long, and the congregation gradually slipped away. The janitor tiptoed up to the pulpit and slipped a note under one corner of the Bible. It read: "When you're through, will you please turn off the lights, lock the door, and put the key under the mat?"

The young minister's first assignment was in a church located at a town famous for its horse racing. He decided his first sermon should be a biting denunciation of gambling and the other evils of the track. After the service one of the members thought he'd confuse the new parson by introducing him to one of the pillars of the church who was, incidentally, the biggest operator at the racetrack. When he heard this, the young pastor was a bit embarrassed.

"I'm afraid I touched on some of your weaknesses," he said, not wishing to offend a generous contributor, "but it was quite unintentional, I assure you."

"It's perfectly alright, sir," said the gambler, "you'd have to preach a mighty weak sermon that wouldn't hit me somewhere!"

"Brethren, I regret to inform you that my dog, who is peculiarly fond of paper, this morning ate that portion of my sermon that I have not delivered. Let us pray."

Visitor: "Pastor, I'd like to know if that dog of yours has any pups. If so, I'd like to get one to give to my minister."

His sermon had already lasted an hour and a half and was about the minor prophets. The preacher said, "And Habbakuk, where shall we put him?"

A man rose in the back row and said, "He can have my seat."

"Pastor, your house is on fire!" hollered a neighbor.

Pastor: "Yes, I know."

"Well, aren't you going to do anything about it?"

"I am. Ever since the fire started, I been praying for rain."

"Lord, send the unfortunate people of this community such sustenance as they sorely need. Send them a truck-load of bread, and a barrel of salt, Lord, and a barrel of pepper...no, Lord, that's too much pepper."

Pastor: "Friend, do you know what each day relentlessly brings nearer?"

Man: "Yes—pay day."

A preacher walked into a bar and ordered a glass of milk and by mistake was served a milk punch.

After drinking it, the holy man lifted his eyes to heaven and was heard to say, "O Lord, what a cow!"

"What a delightful baby!" said the nervous young minister. "And how old is he, she, or it, as the case may be?"

"Just five weeks, Pastor," replied the proud mother.

"Well, well!" said the minister. "Your youngest, I suppose?"

In the middle of his sermon an usher handed the minister a note from an unknown party that simply stated, "Fool."

The minister said, "I have heard of men who wrote letters and forgot to sign their names, but until now, I have never seen one who signed his name and forgot to write the letter."

An English bishop received the following note from the vicar of a village in his diocese:

"I regret in inform you of the death of my wife. Can you possibly send me a substitute for the weekend?"

A retired pastor wrote a letter to his former congregation, "Dear Friends: I will not address you as ladies and gentleman, because I know you so well."

A clergyman was preaching on the subject of future punishment.

"Yes, my brethren," said he, "there is a hell; but…(looking at his watch) "since it's close to noon, we won't go into that just now."

Two men of God came to an inn late one bitter cold night. Exhausted, the elder of the two said a short prayer and climbed quickly into bed. The other man said: "You didn't pray very long." The elder replied: "No, I keep prayed up."

The preacher took a mighty swing at the golf ball and instead of it sailing down the fairway, it dribbled about twelve feet. He frowned, glared and bit his lip, but said nothing.

His opponent regarded him for a moment, and then remarked: "Pastor, that is the most profane silence I have ever witnessed."

At a funeral the pastor said: "My brethren, there will be many surprises for you if you reach the kingdom of Heaven. You will look about expecting to find a great many people who won't be there. There will be a great many people there that you had no idea would ever get in. But, the last and greatest surprise of all will be that you got there yourselves!"

"Brethren," said the pastor, "because of distractions of which you may be aware, I have been unable to compose any sermon to deliver to you this evening. I shall have only to say to you what the Lord will put in my mouth. By next Sunday, I trust to come better prepared."

Man: "Who was Cains wife?"

Not having the answer the preacher said: "I honor every seeker after knowledge of the truth. But I have a word of warning for this questioner. Don't risk losing salvation by too much inquiring after other men's wives."

2

Bringing in the Sheeps (Kids)

Prayed for his mother also—A little boy was sent to bed without supper as punishment, with instructions to pray that he might be a better boy in the future and that his temper might be calmed. His mother crept to the door of his room to make sure that her commands were carried out, and this is the prayer that she heard, "Oh Lord, please take away my bad temper, and while you're at it you might as well take Mother's."

His prayer—Five-year-old Eddie had a small sister who had been seriously ill with pneumonia. After days of anxious watching, the doctor joyfully announced to the family, "Sarah has normal temperature today." Again and again throughout the day he had the same word to give, to the relief and delight of the family. When Eddie said his prayer at bedtime that night he prayed, "God bless mother, father, grandmother and grandfather, and please give them all normal temperatures."

Greater faith hath no man than this—The four-year-old girl was told to pray for her absent father, for her small brother who was ill and for the servant who had a sprained ankle. To her mother's astonishment, the girl finished her prayer as follows: "And now, God, please take good care of yourself, for if anything happens to you we'll all be in big trouble."

God bless her!—A clergyman's small daughter was sent to bed early as punishment just before her father's return from a short trip. Hearing him enter some time later, she called down, "Mama, I want to see Daddy."

There was no response from below.

"Mama, please let Daddy bring me a drink of water."

When that too failed, a small white figure came to the head of the stairs and said sternly, "Mrs. Hastings, I am a very sick woman. I must see my pastor at once."

Needless to say, the pastor went up.

Theology in reverse—On one of his calls the pastor was being entertained by nine-year-old Elizabeth. When there was a lull in the conversation, the minister tried to quiz the little girl. "What are the sins of omission?" he asked.

"Oh, I know," Elizabeth answered. "They're the sins we ought to have committed, but haven't."

No sinners—On a visit to the cemetery one day little Audrey was showing her mother how well she had learned to read by reading aloud from the tombstones. She soon stopped, a puzzled frown on her face.

"What's the matter, dear?" asked her mother. "Did you find one you can't read?"

"No, Mother," replied Audrey, "but I was just wondering. Don't they ever bury sinners?"

Poor example—JUNIOR: "Dad, did you go to Sunday school when you were a little boy?"

DAD (smugly): "I sure did. Never missed a Sunday."

JUNIOR (turning to his mother): "You see, Mom. It won't do me any good either."

Making it all right—A little boy was in the habit of telling tall tales. One day he came into the house and told his mother that there was a bear in the backyard.

His mother said, "Now you know that was just a big dog. You'd better go upstairs and pray to God to forgive you for telling tales."

After the little boy came downstairs his mother asked him if he had prayed to God as she told him to.

"Yes," he said, "and God said it was okay because when He first saw it in the backyard he thought it was a bear too."

Beth's interpretation—Five-year-old Beth had accompanied her older sister to Sunday School for the first time. The lesson that day was about the Commandments. When Beth returned home her mother asked what she had learned at Sunday School.

"Well," little Beth said, "the teacher said we must not witness our bare neighbors."

Getting even—The little girl was being punished and was made to eat her dinner alone at a little table in a corner of the dining room. The rest of the family paid no attention to her until they heard her saying her own private grace: "I thank Thee, Lord, for preparing a table before me in the presence of mine enemies."

Hard question—WILLIE: "Dad, my Sunday School teacher says we're here to help others."
DAD: "Yes, that's so."
WILLIE: "Well, what are the others here for?"

In their steps—"See here now, Peter," said a father to his little son who was misbehaving. "If you're naughty you won't go to heaven."
"I don't want to go to heaven," sobbed the boy, "I want to go with you and mother."

Rather precocious—"Why doesn't the baby talk?" inquired the curious little girl.
"He can't talk yet. Small babies never do."
"Oh yes they do," was the quick answer. "Job did. Nanny read to me out of the Bible how Job cursed the day he was born."

One reason—A teacher asked, "Why did Aaron make a golden calf?"
A bright little farm girl answered, "Because he didn't have enough gold to make a cow."

Poor little fellow!—Mother was showing little Timmy a picture of Christians being thrown to the lions. She talked to him very solemnly about it, trying to make him feel what a terrible thing it was. Then she asked him what he thought about the picture.
"Oh, it's very sad, Mama," said Timmy. "Just look at that poor little lion over in the corner. He doesn't have anything to eat!"

No applause—Little Benjamin was attending a Sunday School entertainment night, and when others applauded for the performances, he thoroughly enjoyed clapping his hands. At the close of the program the minister offered prayer. When he finished, Benjamin noticed there was no applause and piped out shrilly, "He didn't do very well, did he Mama?"

How did he get by?—A little girl who had been besieging her grandfather with an endless succession of questions during the evening had still one more question to ask before she went to bed.

"Granddad," she said, "were you in the ark?"

"Why, no!" he exclaimed smiling.

"But," she said, regarding him with innocent wonder, "then why didn't you drown?"

Nearing heaven—A very small country boy was in the big city for the first time. Taking an elevator to the top of a skyscraper, they shot up thirty stories at breathtaking speed. The little boy, grasping his father's hand, asked timidly, "Daddy, does God know we're coming?"

Naughty Grandpa—A little boy talking to his grandpa suddenly asked, "Grandpa, are you a real good man?"

"I certainly hope so," replied Grandpa, "why do you ask?"

"Well, I had a dream last night. I dreamed I went to heaven and St. Peter said, 'Come right in, little boy, but first you have to write down on a blackboard all the bad things you have done.' And I said, 'All right.' And you were there, Grandpa, writing on blackboards with others, and St. Peter sent me back home for some chalk. I had to go down a ladder to get home, and when I got the chalk and was going up the ladder, I met you, Grandpa, coming down."

"You met me going down the ladder?" said Grandpa, astonished. "What was I going down the ladder for?"

"For more chalk."

Discerning—"Daisy," remarked her teacher, "you shouldn't love your cat too much. What would you do if it died? You won't see it again."

"Oh, yes, I will. I'll see it in heaven."

"No, dear, animals can't go to heaven like people."

Daisy's eyes filled with tears, but suddenly she exclaimed triumphantly, "Animals do go to heaven, for the Bible says the Promised Land is flowing with milk and honey, and if there are no animals where do they get the milk?"

He gave up—The little son of a Baptist minister was very interested one Sunday as his father baptized some new members by immersion. The next morning the young boy proceeded to baptize his three cats in the bathtub. The first two cats tolerated the dunking fairly well, but the old family cat rebelled. She struggled with the boy, clawed him and got away. He caught her again and proceeded with the ceremony. But the old cat acted worse than ever, clawing at him, spitting and scratching his face and hands. Finally he threw her on the floor in disgust and said, "Well, be a Methodist if you want to."

He knew two verses—It was visitors' day in Sunday School, and the teacher called on her brightest pupil to recite a verse from Scripture to impress the visiting dignitaries.

"'And Judas went out and hanged himself,'" said the boy, an impish light in his eyes.

The teacher looked scandalized. The visitor raised his eyebrows and asked, "Do you know another verse, young man?"

"Oh, yes, sir. 'Go thou and do likewise,'" said the boy innocently.

Illustrating the story—The Sunday School superintendent repeated to the children the text, "'Arise, and take the young child and his mother and flee Egypt.'" Then he showed the children a large picture illustrating this text in bright colors.

"Isn't this a nice picture?" he asked. "Here is the mother, here's baby Jesus. There's Egypt in the distance. Isn't that nice?"

The children, however looked disappointed and finally a little boy piped out, "Teacher, where's the flea?"

Watch—A young boy desperately wanted a watch, but was told by his parents that he was a bit too young. He continued to beg for a watch until the whole family was tired of hearing about it. Finally his father explained to him that he would certainly get a watch when he was older, and forbade him from mentioning the subject again. The next Sunday the children of the family were asked to recited Bible verses at the breakfast table. When it was the boy's turn he astonished them all by saying, "What I say unto you I say unto all, 'Watch.'"

False note—A pretty young schoolteacher by the name of Mary Murphy was teaching her class to recite together the twenty-third Psalm. As the young voices repeated the words she thought she heard a mistake. She made the children recite the Psalm individually until at last she came to a little boy who was concluding the Psalm with these words, "Surely good Miss Murphy shall follow me all the days of my life."

Lonesome spot—A little boy was talking to his mother and asked, "Mother, are there any liars in heaven?"

"Certainly not, Brian, how could you think such a thing?"

"Well, all I've got to say is it must be lonesome there with only God and George Washington."

Glad he stopped praying—Little Bobby, who for some months had ended his bedtime prayer with, "Please send me a baby brother," announced to his mother that he was tired of praying for what he did not get, and that he thought God probably didn't have any more little boys to send.

Not long afterward he was carried into his mother's room very early in the morning to see twin boys who had arrived in the night. Bobby looked at the two babies critically, and then remarked, "It's a good thing I stopped praying or there'd have been three of them."

Seems logical—"William," said the Sunday School teacher, "can you tell me what we must do before we can expect forgiveness of sins?"

"Yes," replied the boy, "we must sin."

Concern for the calf—Little Bobby was told the story of the prodigal son. At the end, he burst into tears.

"What's the matter, Bobby," exclaimed his mother.

"I'm so sorry for the poor little calf," he sobbed. "He didn't do anything!"

Bad start—Denise had returned from her first day at Sunday School. Her father asked, "What did my little angel learn this morning?"

"That I'm a child of Satan," was the beaming reply.

Perfect!—A clergyman, while testing a number of students in a class, asked one of them for a definition of matrimony. One boy replied, "A place of punishment where some souls suffer for a time before they can go to heaven."

"Good boy," said the clergyman, "take your seat."

Improving inspiration—The minister was writing his sermon for the following Sunday. His little son was an attentive witness. The minister found it necessary to change several sentences, and would carefully erase and rewrite something on nearly every page of the manuscript. Finally the little fellow asked, "Papa, does God tell you what to say in your sermon?"

"Yes, my son," replied the father, "I always pray that the Lord will guide me."

"Then," replied the boy, "what do you want to go and change it for?"

Had heard him before—A minister was entertaining a couple of clergymen friends at dinner. The guests praised the sermon their host had delivered the Sunday before. The host's son was at the table, and one of the visitors asked him, "My lad, what did you think of your father's sermon?"

"I guess it was very good," said the boy, "but there were three mighty fine places where he could have stopped."

Missionary field—A New York businessman visiting Salt Lake City strolled about and met a little Mormon girl. "I'm from New York," he said to her. "I suppose you don't even know where New York is."

"Oh, yes I do," came the eager reply. "We sent a missionary there."

Horrible surprise—"I've had some terrible disappointments in my years," said the old man, "but none stands out like the one that came to me when I was a boy."

"And what was that?"

"I crawled under a tent to see a circus and discovered it was a revival meeting."

Revised sermons—David was a small boy, the son of a popular preacher. One day his teacher asked, "David, does your father ever preach the same sermons over again?"

"Yes, ma'am," replied David, "but he hollers in different places."

Quite sure—A young boy asked another youngster if he knew what a niche in a church meant. "Well," answered his companion, "an itch in a church is just the same as any other itch, only it is harder to scratch."

Much speaking—A traveler was crossing the country, and being unable to reach a town by night, found lodging with a pious farmer. The next morning the farmer assembled the household for family worship, the stranger being invited to join them. A long chapter was read from the Bible, then all knelt in prayer. The farmer prayed and prayed, continuing for so long that the traveler's knees began to ache and he became very restless. Kneeling near him was the farmer's little boy. The traveler whispered to him, "Is your father about through?"

The boy raised his head, listened a minute, then asked, "Has he said anything about Jesus yet?"

"No," was the reply.

"Well," said the boy, "when he gets there he is just about halfway through."

Reminder—Edward, saying his prayers, said, "And, God, please make Billy stop throwing stones at me. By the way, Lord, I've mentioned this before."

A little flattery now and then—Brenda was fond of waiting at the door of the church and complimenting the priest on his sermon. One day, after Brenda had spread the flattery a bit too thick, the priest remarked "Now, Brenda, you know that your compliments fall off me like water off a duck's back."

Brenda then replied, "Yes, Father, but the ducks like it."

Progress—Two little girls were comparing progress in their catechism class. "I've got to original sin," said one. "How far have you gotten?"

"Oh, I'm way past redemption," the other one answered.

Quick thinking—Coming home one Sunday afternoon with a string of trout, Johnnie saw the minister. There was no way of escape, but the boy rose to the occasion, "Minister, do you see what the trout got for nabbin' worms on Sunday?"

The truth wanted—TOMMY: "Dad, my Sunday School teacher says if I'm good I'll go to heaven."

DAD: "Yes, that's true. What's the problem with that?"

TOMMY: "Well you said if I were good I'd go to the circus. Now I want to know who's telling the truth."

Very reasonable question—Scotty was confused. "Say, Dad, the teacher in Sunday School told us about the evil spirits entering the swine."

"Yes, Scotty, did you have a question about that?"

"I want to know, Dad, if that was the way we got the first deviled ham?"

Getting it right—Two young boys were discussing musical instruments.

"When I grow up, I'm going to get me a eucalyptus," said the first boy.

"A what?" asked the other.

"A eucalyptus. That's a musical instrument, fool."

"Oh, you can't fool me. That's one of the books of the Bible."

No second chance wanted—Tommy was being examined in the catechism by the minister. "What is meant by regeneration?" asked the minister.

"It means to be born again," replied Tommy.

"And would you like to be born again?"

Tommy kept silent for a long time, until finally in desperation the truth came out, "I ain't taking any chances on being a girl!"

Why she asked—Little Mary, seven years old, was saying her prayers. "And, God," she petitioned at the close, "make seven times six be forty-eight."

"But, Mary, why did you say that?" asked her mother.

"Because that's the answer I gave on my math test today and I want it to be right."

He did his best—The minister couldn't be present one Sunday, so he invited a brother minister to preach in his absence. After the morning service the visitor was a guest at the parsonage. One member of the family, a lad about six years old, approached the speaker and asked, "What were you doing in my daddy's pulpit this morning?"

The response was, "Trying to preach." Upon which the lad quietly remarked, "You couldn't quite make it, could you?"

She could name a few—Like most ministers' families, they were as poor as church mice. The little girl was the youngest of ten children until her father explained to her that a baby sister had come in the night.

"Well," she said, after giving it some thought, "I suppose it's all right, Papa, but there's many things we needed worse."

No precaution neglected—The little son of a clergyman appeared at breakfast one morning with obvious signs of getting ready in a hurry. "Why, Eddie," his mother scolded, "I believe you forgot to comb your hair!"

"I was in a hurry to get to school," he explained.

"I hope you didn't forget to say your prayers?" she asked anxiously.

"No, ma'am!" was his emphatic reply. "That's one thing I never forget. Safety first!"

A temptation to move—A pastor received a call from a church that was much larger and would pay considerably more than the church he was currently serving. He replied that he would prayerfully consider the matter and give his answer in a short time. The pastor's little boy was down at the grocery store of one of the members and was asked if his father had decided whether to take the new church. The little boy replied, "I don't know. Papa is still praying about the matter, but we have all the things about packed."

Bless her heart!—Dorothy overheard her parents talking about Bible names. "Is my name in the Bible?" she asked.

"No, dear."

"Why not? Didn't God make me?"

"Yes, dear."

"Then why didn't he say something about it?"

He knew his lesson—The teacher was talking of kindness to animals, and telling her pupils to be kind to them always. "I once saw a little boy cut the tail off a cat. Can anybody tell me a passage of Scripture where such a thing is forbidden?"

The brightest boy of the class answered, "What God has joined together, let no man put asunder."

Dad was an artist!—Johnny was in the habit of swearing mildly when anything did not please him. One day the minister heard him and said, "Johnny, don't you know you must not swear? It is naughty of you. Why, every time I hear you swear, a cold chill runs down my spine."

"That's nothing," said Johnny. "If you'd been here at the house the other day when Dad hammered his thumb, you'd have frozen to death."

He omitted the quotation marks—A clergyman told his daughter a bedtime story every evening before she went to sleep. One night he told her such a thrilling tale that the child looked very straight at her father and asked, "Daddy, is that a true story or are you preaching?"

Self-service—One six-year-old girl spent the evening playing with her new alphabet blocks until 9:00 when she was taken to bed. She was very drowsy, almost falling asleep when she remembered that she had not said her prayers. She turned, pushed the blocks with a vague gesture, and said sleepily, "Oh Lord, I'm too sleepy to pray. There are the blocks; spell it out for yourself."

Taking no chances—Little Donny's birthday was approaching and the one thing he wanted more than anything else in the world was a large red fire truck. So he incorporated this wish into his evening prayers.

"And please, dear God, send me a red fire truck for my birthday," he shouted at the top of his lungs.

"But, Donny," his mother protested, "you don't have to shout like that. God isn't deaf, you know."

"No," agreed Donny, "but Granny is."

Another time—One evening the young minister who had been courting Grace, the oldest daughter, was dining with the family. Marie, the little sister, was talking rapidly when the visitor was about to ask the blessing.

Turning to the child, he said in a polite voice, "Marie, I'm going to ask grace."

"Well, it's about time," promptly answered the little girl, "we've been expecting it nearly a year, and she has too."

Natural plea—As little Chris ended his prayer he fervently prayed, "And please, God, put the vitamins in pie and cake instead of in cauliflower and spinach. Amen."

Not the Lord's responsibility—A well-known minister in a suburban town was going away for several days. When saying good-bye to his family, he took Bobby up in his arms with the remark, "Well, young man, I want you to be a good boy and be sure to take good care of Momma."

Bobby promised, and all day kept a sharp eye on his mother. That evening when saying his prayers, he asked, "Oh, Lord, please protect Papa and Brother Dick and Sister Alice and Aunt Mary, and all the little Jones boys, and me. But you needn't trouble about Momma, for I am going to look after her myself."

True to form—A lad of six was invited over to lunch in a neighbor's home. As soon as all were seated at the table, the food was served. The little boy was puzzled. With the frankness of a child, he asked the host, "Don't you say any prayer before you eat?"

The host was very uncomfortable and mumbled, "No, we don't take time for that."

The lad thought silently for a while and then said, "You're just like my dog! You start right in."

Loud speaking—A sincere and devout minister had an unfortunate habit of bellowing. He was especially loud during his public prayers. After one of his loud prayers, during which the rafters were almost vibrating, a little girl whispered to her father, "Father, don't you think if he lived nearer to God he wouldn't have to talk so loud?"

The difference—Mother was very careful indeed about the upbringing of little Tommy. She was especially careful to make him say grace before each meal.

Recently in a restaurant after the waitress had served the drinks, Mother said to Tommy, "Now say grace, please, Tommy."

Tommy looked up in surprise. "But, Momma," he objected, "we're paying for this, aren't we?"

Lesson learned—The teacher was giving the class a lesson on the evils of drink. She demonstrated this by placing some water in one glass and some liquor in another. With a pair of tweezers she placed a worm in each glass. The worm dropped into the glass of liquor soon puckered up into a shriveled mass, while the one placed in the glass of water swam about seemingly enjoying the bath. The keen interest of the children highly pleased the teacher. She called upon Johnnie to tell the class what he learned from the experiment. Johnnie answered confidently, "If you drink liquor, you won't have worms."

Just depends—"Do you say your prayers every night, young man," asked the pastor.

"Naw," the youngster replied, "some nights I don't want nothin'."

A child's advice—One morning a Sunday School was about to be dismissed and the children were already in anticipation of relaxing their cramped limbs. The superintendent arose and, instead of the usual dismissal, announced, "Now, children, let me introduce Mr. Smith, who will give us a short talk."

Mr. Smith arose and, after gazing impressively around the classroom, began with, "I hardly know what to say." A small voice back in the rear lisped, "Thay amen and thit down!"

Pray as you go—We should not ask God to answer prayers that we could answer ourselves, because He will not do it. Two little girls were hurrying to school and were afraid they would be tardy. Said one, "Let's kneel right down and pray that we won't be tardy."

But the other gave this common sense reply, "Oh no, let's just hurry on to school and pray while we're goin'."

Resisting temptation—"I met our new minister on the way to Sunday School, mamma," said the small boy, "and he asked me if I ever played marbles on Sunday."

"What did you say to that?" asked his mother.

"I said, 'get thee behind me, Satan,' and walked right off," was the reply.

Qualified—A little girl who had been naughty and had received punishment from her mother, said this prayer fervently when she went to bed that night: "Oh, God, please make me good; not real good, just good enough so I won't have to be punished."

In His image—The little boy was found by his mother with pencil and paper making a sketch. When asked what he was doing he answered promptly and proudly, "I'm drawing a picture of God."

His mother gasped, "But you can't do that. No one has ever seen God. No one knows how God looks."

"Well," the little boy replied cheerfully, "when I get through they will."

Undecided as yet—The little boy, in answer to the question as to what he wanted to be when he grew up, said, "I'll be either a minister or a Christian, but I haven't decided which yet."

Launch out into the deep—Many Christians fail because they don't go forward. A little girl fell out of bed one night. The next morning her mother asked her how it had happened.

"I don't know, Mama," was the reply, "unless I stayed too near the place where I got in."

Stale prayers—Little Jane asked, "Why can't we pray for our bread once a week or once a month? Why must we ask every day for our daily bread?"

Her older sister answered, "So we can have it fresh, silly."

Not needed—Little Harold had a deeply religious and at the same time a most practical nature. On one occasion he climbed the roof of a very steep shed, lost his footing and began to slide swiftly toward the edge of the roof. "Oh, Lord, save me!" he prayed. "Oh, Lord, save me! Oh, Lord! Oh…never mind, I have caught on a nail."

She had him cold—The minister's daughter returned at 3:00 in the morning from a dance. Her father greeted her sternly. "Good morning, child of the devil."

Respectfully and demurely she replied, "Good morning, Father."

Answering your prayers—A little girl prayed that her brother would not catch any birds. Then she prayed that his trap would not catch any birds. Then she kicked the trap to pieces, and it didn't catch any birds.

Kids are the same the world over—Little Billy was dressing to go to Sunday School. He couldn't find his clothes and kept pestering his mother. Finally he was dressed except for his feet. "Momma," he whined, "do you know where my socks and shoes are?"

"Billy!" said his exasperated mother, "Your shoes are behind the door, where you left them, your socks are in the drawer, and your feet are on your body. Now see if you can mingle them!"

A future announcer—Finishing his prayers one night, a young boy surprised his family by saying, "This concludes our program for tonight. Good night and God bless."

Logical—A small boy asked what the Darwinian theory meant, and was shocked by the statement that many people believed that monkeys were the ancestors of man. "But that can't be," he repeated many times in dismay, evidently searching for a more satisfactory answer to this startling theory. Finally his face lit up with a conclusive argument against it. "Don't you see," he said, "some day we shall be ancestors, and we are not monkeys."

Bible knowledge scarce—The Sunday School superintendent said, "We will now read a chapter in unison."

A pupil whispered to his seatmate, "Tell me quick, is unison in the New Testament or in the Old Testament."

Helping dad—A preacher, raising his eyes from the podium in the middle of his sermon, was shocked to see his son in the audience pelting the congregation with peanuts. But while the preacher was preparing to scold the boy, little Jeffrey shouted out, "You keep preaching, Daddy, I'll keep them awake!"

Expecting an answer—"Why are you taking your umbrella? It doesn't look like rain today," said the father to his little girl as they started for church.

"Because I heard you praying for rain this morning," was the reply.

Lead the children—The way to get the children to Sunday School and church is for the parents to go and take the children with them.

Little Tommy didn't want to go to bed. Her mother persuaded with the statement, "Tommy, the little chickens went to bed long ago."

"Yes," said Tommy, "but the old hen went first."

Can't pray over it—A mother wanted her son to go to dance class because he was so awkward. She wanted him to be more graceful, but he was reluctant to go. After six weeks he had made such poor progress she took him out of class in disgust and scolded him. He told her, "I'm sorry, Mother, but I can't seem to do any better. You see, it's one of those things I can't pray over."

Limiting his prayers—Little 7-year-old Joe's mother was proud of his curly hair, but his Uncle Robert was continually teasing him and calling him a girl. One night Joe ended his prayer with: "God bless Mother, God bless Father," when his mother said to him, "Joe, you forgot to ask God to bless Uncle Robert." The boy answered, "Well, God can bless him if he wants to, but he needn't do it to please me."

Taking his time—MOTHER: "Have you said your prayers, Bobby?"
BOBBY: "Yes, Mother."
"And did you ask God to make you a good boy?"
"Yes, Mother—but not yet."

News to her—A traveling salesman one night was stranded in a small town because a bridge had washed out. He turned to the waitress and remarked, "This certainly looks like the Flood."

"The what?"

"The flood. You have read about the Flood, and the Ark landing on Mount Ararat, surely."

"Gee, mister," she replied. "I haven't seen a paper for three weeks!"

Encouraging the preacher—Little Anna's father was a baseball enthusiast and had taken her to several games. One Sunday morning she went with him and her mother to church. Anna wasn't very interested in the sermon until the minister warmed up to his subject and the older men near the pulpit began to shout, "Amen," "Hallelujah," etc. On the way home she looked up at her father and exclaimed, "Say, Dad, who were those men up front rooting for the preacher?"

An exclusive job—Too many people look upon the church and its work like the little boy the minister met on the sidewalk one Sunday morning.

"Are you going to church, Brad?" he asked.

"No, sir," the boy replied.

"Why not? I'm going," said the minister.

"Of course," said Brad, "you've got to go. It's your job."

The real question—Little Beth asked her mother, "How will I know when I've been naughty?"

"Your conscience will tell you, dear."

"I don't care what it tells me," said Beth, "will it tell God?"

It all depends—The teacher had been trying to teach the principles of the Golden Rule and "turn the other cheek."

"Now, Timothy," she asked, "what would you do supposing a boy hit you?"

"How big a boy are you supposing?" demanded Timothy.

Arrange beforehand—A little girl who had been raised in a strict Presbyterian church came to her mother one Saturday afternoon and eagerly asked, "Mother, may I go to the Episcopal church with Ginny tomorrow? I promise not to believe a single word the minister says."

Classed too low—A Methodist minister was making a pastoral call on one of his families, where a little Episcopal girl was playing with the daughter of the family. Congratulating the Methodist girl that she was a Christian, he turned to the other and asked, "Are you a child of God, dear?" She replied with dignity, "No, I'm an Episcopalian."

Variable age—A minister called at a home just after he had come to his new church. The little boy was entertaining him before his mother came downstairs. Trying to be cordial, the preacher said, "How old are you, little man?"

"I am five at home, six at school, and four at the movies," was the frank reply.

Knew his limitations—A small boy, when told by his Sunday School teacher that he would leave his body behind when he died, said in alarm, "I don't understand that!"

"You see," explained the teacher, "you will take all that is good with you to the better land and leave all that is not good here on earth."

"Oh!" he exclaimed. After a moment's thought he added soberly, "I guess I'm going to be pretty thin up there, teacher."

More than enough—An 8-year-old boy went to the church picnic and, being a favorite with the ladies, was liberally supplied with good things to eat. Later in the day one of the ladies noticed the boy sitting near the stream with a sick expression on his face and hands clasped over his stomach.

"What's the matter, Justin?" she kindly asked. "Haven't you had enough to eat?"

"Oh, yes ma'am," said the boy. "I've had enough. I feel as though I don't want all I've got."

Dusty Bibles—The pastor in making his calls found little Mary crying. "Now what is the matter with my little girl?" he asked consolingly.

"Mama got my apron all dirty," she sobbed.

"And how did your mama happen to get your apron dirty?"

"When she saw you coming she took it to wipe the dust off the Bible."

Righteous indignation—At Sunday School the children were asked to explain the meaning of "righteous indignation." One young man answered, "Being angry without swearing."

Remember the text—A little boy went to church and heard the sermon, "Fear not, the comforter cometh." When he got home, someone asked if he remembered what the preacher talked about and he replied, "Yes, it was: Don't worry, you'll get your quilt back."

Too common—A little boy was taught the Lord's prayer, and for a few days he said it faithfully and proudly. One day, however, he announced to his mother in disgust, "I heard another fellow saying that prayer today. It's going to get all over town!"

R-R-R-Revenge!—Little Jack had been persistently naughty, so his mother gave him a good spanking. The rest of the afternoon a desire for revenge burned in his little heart.

Soon bedtime came, and kneeling down, he said his evening prayer, asking a blessing for all the members of the family individually—except one. Rising, he turned to his mother with a triumphant look and said, "I suppose you noticed you weren't in it!"

A pleasant parable—Little Justin was asked if he ever studied the Bible. "Yes, sir," he replied.

"Then of course you know all about the parables," said the questioner. "Yes, sir," said Justin.

"Good! Will you tell me which parable you like the best?" "I like the one where everybody loafs and fishes," said Justin.

Children know—"Mama," said the little girl, her eyes wide with excitement, "I think the minister told a tall tale!"

"You shouldn't say such a thing!" replied the mother.

"But he did, Mama! Papa asked him how long he had worn a beard, and Pastor said he's worn them all his life."

Feed the sheep and get more wool—A clergyman famous for his fundraising ability was teaching a Sunday School. When comparing himself as a pastor of the church to a shepherd and his congregation to the sheep, he asked the following question to the children. "What does the shepherd do for the sheep?" To the confusion of the minister a small boy in the front row piped out, "Shears them!"

Beyond him—The siblings had quarreled all day. After an early supper mother tried to re-establish family unity, finally quoting the Bible verse, "Let not the sun go down upon your anger." Turning to the older boy, she said, "Now, Bradley, are you going to let the sun go down on your anger?" Bradley squirmed as he looked into her pleading face.

"Well, how can I stop it?" he questioned.

The power of example—A father came home one evening and found little Janie and Johnny pulling each other's hair, pushing and shoving, with toys scattered all over the floor.

"What's the matter? Stop that fighting this minute!" he demanded.

"Oh, we're not fighting," was the reply.

"Then what in the world are you doing?"

"We're just playing Mother and Father."

One thing I know—A person may not be highly educated or rich, but he can have salvation and know it. A man who was driving across an isolated part of the country encountered a young boy and asked him, "How far to Goodland?"

The boy replied, "I don't know."

"How far is it to Oakley?"

"Don't know."

"What county is this?"

"I don't know the name."

Frustrated, the stranger said, "You're not very smart, are you?"

The boy replied, "No, but I ain't lost."

"Now I lay me down to sleep,
I pray the Lord my soul to keep.
When he hollers let him go,
Eenie, meenie, miny, mo."

Mom: "You prayed to God to bless Momma, Papa, and Grandma, why didn't you ask him to bless Aunt Jane also?"

Kid: "I didn't think it would be polite to ask for so much all at once."

"And dear Lord, please send the beautiful snow to keep the little flowers warm through the winter."

"Hey, Mom. I fooled God. I really wanted the snow so I can go sledding."

Mom: "You've been naughty. Go to your room and pray to God that you will be better."

Later: "Did you pray that you would be good?"

Kid: "Na, I told God to help you put up with me."

Because of bad table manners, Bobby was punished and sent to eat in the corner by himself.

He prayed: "I thank thee, Lord, for preparing for me a table in the presence of mine enemies."

Preacher: "Do you say your prayers at night?"

Boy: "Yes, sir."

Preacher: "Do you say them in the morning, too?"

Boy: "Na, I'm not scared in the daytime."

One child said, "Mom, I don't mind going to Sunday School any other day, but it just spoils Sunday."

This little boy wasn't known for paying attention during church but one day after playing hard he grabbed his side and said, "Mom, I've got a bad pain. You don't suppose I'm going to have a wife do you?"

Mom: "What are you children doing?"

Kid: "We're playing church."

Mom: "But, why are you whispering?"

Kid: "We're the choir."

Boy: "I think I'll be a preacher when I grow up."

Dad: "That would be great. Why did you decide that?"

Boy: "I figured since I had to go to church anyway, I might as well stand up and holler get paid for it instead of sitting still in the pew."

1st boy: "Why don't you come with me to my church?"

2nd boy: "'Cause I belong to another abomination."

Boy: "I don't see why you asked another blessing on supper, Dad. It's the same stuff we had last night."

Dad: "Did you behave in church?"

Kid: "Yes, sir, I sure did. I even heard a lady sitting behind me say she'd never seen a child behave so."

The little boy was saying his bedtime prayers:

Mom: "I can't hear you, dear."

Boy: "I wasn't talking to you."

God bless Mamma.
God bless Papa.
God bless Freddie,
Rah! Rah! Rah!

Mom: "Don't forget to include Grandma in you prayers tonight and ask God to let her live to be very, very old."

Kid: "Oh, she's old enough. I'd rather pray that God would make her young."

Little girl: "Will I get everything I pray for, Mom?"

Mom: "Everything that's good for you."

Little girl: "What's the use, then. I get that anyway."

Preacher: 'Do you say your prayers every night?"

Kid: "Na, some nights I don't want nothin'".

Kid: "And God bless Grandma and Grandpa and make them happy…if they're not too old for that sort of thing."

Preacher: 'And what does you Mom do for you when you've been good?"

Kid: "She lets me stay home from church."

Preacher: "Could you forgive a boy for hitting you?"

Kid: "I could if he was a lot bigger than I am."

"Dear Lord, I know I'm a bad little girl, and I do wish you would help me to be better, and if at first you don't succeed, try, try again."

Mom: "Now, Lucy, say your prayers and ask God to make you well."

Lucy: "Isn't that what we're paying the doctor for?"

Preacher addressing a Sunday School class: "Well, children, what shall I speak about?"
Kid: "What do you know?"

Priest: "I see you are a bright little man. And how high can you count?"
Boy: "One, two, three, four, five, six, seven, eight, nine, ten, Jack, Queen, and King!"

3

The Chosen (The Flock)

So long—In a New England town noted for its stormy and blustering citizens, a clergyman told his friend, "We have just had the greatest revival our church has experienced for many years."

"I'm glad to hear it," replied the friend. "And how many did you add to the fold?"

"We didn't add any," said the clergyman, "but we got rid of three."

Immersion not so practical—The mayor of a tough frontier town was about to engage a preacher for the new church. "Pardon, you aren't by any chance a Baptist, are you?" the mayor asked.

"Oh, no. Why?"

"Well, I was just going to say we have to haul our water twelve miles."

Locating Jonah—Bishop Carpenter, while addressing an open-air meeting, was asked by an atheist if he believed that Jonah was swallowed by the whale.

"When I get to heaven I will ask Jonah," said the Bishop.

"What if he isn't there?" the atheist persisted.

"Then you will have to ask him," was the quick retort.

Special prayer—"Pastor, I'd like you to pray for me. I'm in a bad way, sir," said Randolph to his pastor.

"Well, Randolph, what's wrong with you?" asked the minister.

"I've got a floating kidney, sir."

"But, Randolph, I can't pray for physical things like that. I only pray for spiritual things."

"You can't pray for a floating kidney? Then how come you prayed last Sunday for them loose livers?"

Terminal facilities needed—The minister who was noted for his long, rambling sermons at last reached something of a resting place in his talk. Pausing to take a breath he asked the question, "And what shall I say next?"

A voice from the congregation responded with an emphatic, "Amen!"

Helping out the weak—Deacons Smith and Jones, two pillars of the church, were walking along the riverbank on a hot summer afternoon. Suddenly Deacon Smith called out excitedly, "What's this I found in the river?"

"Looks to me like a jug of liquor!" Deacon Jones responded, his eyes wide.

Both deacons were quiet and solemn for a moment, then Deacon Smith said gravely, "Brother Jones, don't you think we'd better drink up this liquor before some poor, weak brother finds it and falls by the wayside?"

Fulfilling expectations—The cheerful visitor tried to persuade old widow Barnes not to dwell upon her troubles, telling her she would feel happier if she ignored them.

"I don't know about that," replied the old woman. "I always figured that when the Lord sends me tribulation he expects me to tribulate."

In memorial—"I presume you carry a memento of some kind in that locket you wear?" the clergyman's wife asked the parishioner.

"Yes, ma'am," the woman replied. "It's a lock of my husband's hair."

"But your husband is still alive!" she exclaimed.

"Yes, but his hair is gone."

Disconcerting—A dignified old woman, ascending the steps of the church, had difficulty climbing all those stairs and asked the rector's assistance. He offered his arm, and, on reaching the church door she thanked him and inquired, "Do you happen to know who is preaching this morning?"

"The rector, madam," the rector replied.

"Oh," she said, "then might I beg you to do me another favor? Would you be good enough to assist me down the steps again?"

Not her husband—At the funeral service of a church member, the minister made a glowing tribute to the virtues of the deceased. The man had not lived a very exemplary life. He was known as a drinker, a gambler, a loafer, and a generally worthless individual. The minister, however, pictured him entirely differently, describing him as a loving father and husband, a worthy citizen, and a faithful member of the church.

The widow listened intently, then nudging her little boy, whispered, "Timmy, you slip over and peek in that coffin and see if that's your daddy in there."

A treacherous memory—The preacher admonished his parishioner, "You must never hold on to a grudge against your neighbor, Brother Jackson. If your neighbor does you an injury, you must forget it."

"Oh, I do forget it, Preacher. But I've got a powerfully bad memory, and I keep forgetting that I forgot it."

A working spirit—A minister called on an old woman and found her bending over the washtub, scrubbing with all her might. "Don't you get very tired doing all that hard work?" he asked kindly.

"Oh, yes, sir," she replied. "I haven't got much strength. But I ask the Lord and he gives me the spirit of washing."

So she can gnash—An evangelist was exhorting his listeners to flee from the wrath to come. "I warn you," he thundered, "there will be weeping and wailing and gnashing of teeth!"

At that moment an old woman stood up. "Sir," she shouted, "I have no teeth."

"Madam," returned the evangelist, "teeth will be provided."

Her responsibility—"Susan," asked the preacher, "do you take this man to be your wedded husband for better or for worse?"

"Just as he is, Parson," she answered. "If he gets any better I'll know the good Lord's going to take him, and if he gets any worse, why, I'll tend to him myself."

Meddling—As the preacher was preaching fervently against all the common sins ranging from murder to cheating on a tax return, a devout old woman swayed and rocked in her pew, murmuring, "Amen. Amen. Praise God!" Then the preacher started on the subject of Bingo gambling, at which the woman sat bolt upright and muttered to herself, "Now he's stopped preachin' and took to meddlin'."

It seemed that way—A poor man had five children and his wife presented him with twins. The minister met him on the street and said, "I see the Lord has smiled on you again."

"Smiled," said the poor man, "he laughed right out loud."

Rapid advancement—A minister taught an illiterate man in his parish how to read. The man proved to be quite intelligent and a quick learner. After the tutoring had come to an end the minister was not able to call at the man's home for several months. One night he dropped by and was met at the door by the man's wife. "How is John?" asked the minister.

"Quite well, sir," replied the wife.

"How does he get along with his reading?"

"Very nicely, thank you."

"Wonderful! I suppose he is able to read his Bible easily now?"

"Bible, sir? Why he was out of the Bible and into the newspaper long ago!"

Playing the game—In a New England village, where the Sunday church attendance was small, lived a young widow who had taken a fancy to the minister. She could see that he also cared for her, but was evidently too shy to say anything. One Sunday the congregation was smaller than usual. After the service the clergyman said to the widow, "Did you like my sermon?"

"It was beautiful," she replied.

"I wish more people would come," he said.

She saw her chance. "So do I," she answered. "Why, tonight, every time you said 'dearly beloved' I started blushing!"

Enlargement unnecessary—The space in the cemetery had become filled up to such an extent that it was proposed to buy the adjoining plot of ground in order to have more room. An old brother objected, "I have measured the yard and have counted all our members. I find that there is just enough room left to bury all our members without buying any more land."

He caught them—The minister announced, "Next Sunday I'm going to preach on the subject of lying. As preparation for my sermon, I'd like each of you to read the seventeenth chapter of Mark." The following Sunday the preacher rose to begin, and asked, "All of you who read the seventeenth chapter of Mark this past week, please raise your hands." Almost half the congregation raised their hands. Then the preacher said, "Very good, you are the people I want to talk to. There is no seventeenth chapter of Mark."

The eternal libel—"No man can serve two masters," said the minister to one of his parishioners.

"Oh, I know all about that, Pastor. My brother tried it and now he's doing time for bigamy."

For self-preservation—A mission worker tells of a woman who stood up to testify to her conversion at a Salvation Army meeting. She said, "I was very foolish and vain. Worldly pleasure, especially the fashions, were my only thought. I was fond of silks, satins, jewelry, ribbons, and laces. But, my friends, when I found that they were dragging me down to eternal suffering, I gave them all to my sister."

One simple solution—"Jeremy, the widow Decker tells me that you stole one of her pigs. Is that correct?"

"Yes, your reverence."

"What have you done with it?"

"Killed it and ate it, your reverence."

"Oh, Jeremy, that was evil! When you are brought face to face with the widow and the pig on Judgment Day, what will you be able to say for yourself when the widow accuses you of stealing?"

"Did you say the pig would be there, sir?"

"Yes, I did."

"Well, then, I'll say, 'Mrs. Decker, there's your pig.'"

Sure proof—DEACON (after an outdoor baptism): "Is the water cold, Sam?"

SAM: "No, not a bit cold."

DEACON: "Better put him under again, elder. He hasn't quit lying yet."

Where faith breaks down—Many pastors will say that religious skepticism is due to misunderstanding the Bible. A businessman once said to his minister, "Pastor, I can believe the story of the ark. I can accept the ark's enormous size, its odd shape, and the vast number of animals it contained. But when I'm asked to believe that the children of Israel carried this contraption around in the wilderness for forty years…well, I have to say my faith breaks down."

Better bargain—The preacher was annoyed by an old man who fell asleep during his sermon for several consecutive Sundays. The old man usually brought his grandson with him and one Sunday after service, the preacher spoke to the boy in the vestry and said, "My good boy, if you will keep your Grandpa awake during the sermon, I will pay you a dollar every week."

This seemed like a good deal to the boy, and for the next two weeks the old man listened attentively. But the third week he dropped off soundly asleep and the minister was upset.

Sending for the boy he asked, "Didn't you agree to keep your Grandpa awake every week for a dollar?"

"Yes, sir," the boy replied, "but now Grandpa pays me two dollars not to disturb him."

Backward look—When the preacher called on his new congregational member, she answered the door wearing heavy mourning clothes. The good man kindly inquired, "Is your husband dead, Ma'am?"

"Oh no, sir, he isn't dead," was the reply.

"Then why are you in mourning," the preacher asked.

"It's like this," explained the woman. "My present husband has been nagging and bothering me so much that I went back into mourning for my first husband."

Just what he wanted—An old man walked into a little crossroads store. "Hello there, Jim," the proprietor greeted him. "I hear that you finally got converted at last night's meeting and have given up drinking."

"Yes, sir, I've seen the error of my ways," Jim declared fervently.

"Well, congratulations. You deserve a great deal of credit for that," the merchant said approvingly.

"Yes, sir, that's just what I thought," Jim said, smiling happily. "And that's why I'm here, to get some of that credit on groceries and fabrics."

A makeshift—"Well, hello there, Matthew. I saw you leaving church today. But I thought you had decided to become a Baptist."

"Yes, sir, I have. But since it's winter I'm being sprinkled into Episcopalian until summer comes."

Shooting close—During a revival, Alan felt moved to stand and give his experience. He was speaking smoothly and sounding quite pious when the parson suddenly interrupted him.

"Mr. Johnson," said the good man, with a no-nonsense look in his eye, "did you ever steal any chickens?"

"No, sir," stated Alan firmly, "I never stole any chickens."

"Good," commented the parson. "Did you ever steal any turkeys?"

"No, sir," answered Alan just as firmly, "I never stole any turkeys either." The parson sat down and Alan was allowed to conclude his experience and was warmly congratulated by the brothers and sisters.

"Golly," said Alan upon leaving the church, "If that parson would have said ducks I surely would have fallen down dead."

Ready to leave—A preacher based his sermon on the prophets. He had taken an hour to talk about the major prophets, then he started on the minor prophets. When he at length came to Hosea he exclaimed, "Brothers and sisters! We now come to Hosea. Let us consider him. Where shall we put Hosea?"

At that moment an old man who had been peacefully sleeping in one of the back pews woke up and looked at the pastor. "Hosea can take my seat," he said. "I'm so doggoned tired that I'm going home."

Reassured—Wallace was remodeling an old church and he and one of the elders were on the job inspecting. There was a plumb line attached to one corner of the roof. The elder was eyeing it with some anxiety and doubt. "Look at that plumb line, Brother," he addressed Wallace, "isn't that building leaning over?"

"Oh, no sir," replied Wallace, thinking fast. "That building's all right. That's just an old plumb line and it ain't reliable, that's all."

Man born to be took—"Do you take this woman to be your lawfully wedded wife?" asked the parson, glancing at the diminutive groom, who stood beside 200 pounds of femininity.

"I take nothin'," gloomily responded the groom. "I'm bein' took."

Old individualist—"Stand up!" shouted the evangelist, "if you want to go to heaven." Everybody stood up but one old man. "Don't you want to go to heaven, my brother?" shouted the preacher.

"Sure," said the old man. "But I ain't going with no excursion."

One excuse for leaving—Pastor: "By the way, Mrs. Smith, I was sorry to see your husband leave church in the middle of the sermon. I trust nothing was seriously the matter with him."

Mrs. Smith: "Oh, no sir, it was nothing serious. But you see, the poor man does have a terrible habit of walking in his sleep."

Not a complaint at all—The good priest had come to his parishioner after the funeral of the latter's mother-in-law to express condolences. "And what complaint was it, Samuel, that carried the dear lady off?" the priest asked sympathetically.

"Complaint?" answered Samuel. "There was no complaint from anybody. Everybody was satisfied."

Did the preacher put them to sleep?—A deacon and his wife shared their pew for many years with a spinster. Shortly after the death of his wife the deacon married the spinster. A witty member of the congregation approached the minister after the wedding and said, "I see you've married the deacon and Miss Jones."

"Yes," said the minister, "and I think it's a good marriage."

"So do I," said the wit. "People who have slept together in the same pew so long ought to be married."

Had become truthful—The traveling salesman spoke to an old man seated in front of the village store. "They say you remember seeing George Washington. Is that right?"

"Well, sir," said the man, "I used to remember seeing him, but I had to forget since I joined the church."

Sins well paid for—A minister discovered two men playing cards on Sunday for money. "Gentlemen!" exclaimed the preacher, "don't you know it's wrong to gamble on the Sabbath?"

"Yes, pastor," answered one man ruefully. "But believe me, I'm paying for my sins!"

Also happened elsewhere—A man in the rear pew of a fashionable church was observed from the pulpit with his hat on. The minister beckoned to a deacon, who went to the man and asked him if he were aware that his hat was on. "Thank God!" said the man. "I thought that would do it. I have attended this church for six months and you are the first one who has spoken to me."

Some will get in—"What is your reason for not going to church?" a new member of the community was asked.

The reply was, "I find so many hypocrites there."

"Don't let that keep you away," replied the questioner, "there is always room for one more."

His sort—Jonathon had been going from one church to another to find a congenial congregation. Finally one Sunday morning he dropped into a little church just as the congregation recited with the minister, "We have left undone those things which we ought to have done; and we have done those things we ought not to have done."

Jonathon dropped into a pew with a sigh of relief and satisfaction. "Praise be!" he said solemnly, "at last I have found my crowd."

Good advice—Don't get angry and threaten to quit the church. A preacher said, "Some folks think they hurt the church when they get mad and quit. But they are wrong about that. It never hurts the tree for the old dried up apples to fall off."

Unconvinced—A country preacher thought very highly of a sermon he had preached on Atheism, and was so proud of it that he asked a man of his congregation how he had liked the sermon.

"Well, sir," came the reply, "for all you said, and no doubt it was very clever, I still believe there is a God."

Setting him straight—The former vicar and his wife decided to attend the church social of his old parish. The new vicar greeted his predecessor heartily. "I'm very pleased to see you again," he said. "And is this your most charming wife?"

"This," the other replied reprovingly, "is my only wife."

Practical—A minister was telling a group of parishioners about the prodigal son. "What would you have done in the prodigal's place? Sleeping with the swine. No home. No friends. No food. I ask you, what would you have done?"

The answer came quickly from a practical-minded man in the last row, "Mister, I would have killed a pig."

Refund wanted—A man called at the minister's home looking as though he had something on his mind. "I just came to ask you," he said, "whether it is right for any person to profit from the mistakes of other people?"

"Most certainly not," replied the minister.

His caller brightened and held out his right hand. "If that's the case," he said, "perhaps you'd return the $40 I gave you last October for marrying me."

A peculiar religion—A man stood up in prayer meeting and testified to the great things the Lord had done for him. He said that before he was converted he worried a great deal over his debts, but now since he had religion he allowed his creditors to do the worrying.

Very biblical—A noted eastern judge visiting in the West went to church on Sunday, knowing beforehand that the preacher was very boring and long winded. After the service the preacher met the judge in the vestibule and said, "Your, Honor, how did you like the sermon?"

"Oh, quite well, quite well," the judge answered kindly. "It was like the peace of God, for it passed all understanding, and like his mercy, I thought it would go on forever."

The needless water—An earnest brother in his prayer said, "Lord, we thank you for the spark of life you have given unto us, and we pray that you will continue to water it."

It works both ways—A minister had just married a couple, and in a jocular way remarked, "It is customary to kiss the bride, but in this instance we will omit it."

Quick as a flash the groom replied, "It is customary for the groom to give the minister a nice fee for performing a ceremony, but in this instance we will also omit that."

Talking too high—A learned professor was invited to lecture to a rural community and talked completely over the heads of the audience. At the close of his lecture, he dropped his lofty style, and blandly remarked, "If anyone has a question to ask, I'll do my best to answer it."

An old farmer in the back seat slowly rose and asked the first and only question, "I would be very much obliged, mister, if you'd just tell us what on earth it is you've been preaching about."

A good member—A preacher was about to take a ride on a horse hired at the livery stable. "That's a fine looking animal," he said to the owner. "Is he as good as he looks?" The owner replied, "That horse will work in any place you put him and do all that any horse can do." The preacher eyed the horsed admiringly and then remarked, "I wish he was a member of my church."

United, all right—A zealous young teacher from a United Brethren church was out looking for new recruits for his Sunday School class. He approached one young man whom he met in the downtown district and gave him an invitation to attend his class.

"I dunno as I ought to," said the lad, "because I can't rightly tell where I do belong. A Methodist woman gave me this coat, a Baptist fellow gave me my pants, a Presbyterian guy gave me the shoes and a Reformed young woman my hat."

"Oh," interrupted the young teacher, "then of course you are a United Brethren! You just come along with me."

Better than no excuse—"I'm glad to see you come so regularly to our evening services, Mrs. Brown," said the minister.

"Thank you. You see, my husband hates me going out in the evening, so I do it to spite him."

He wanted an understanding—A village clergyman, going the rounds of his parish one day, met an old parishioner. "Hello, George," the parson said. "How come you haven't been in church for several Sundays?"

"I don't have any Sunday trousers," replied George.

"Oh, I can remedy that," said the parson. "I have a pair at the house that will fit you. I'll send them over today."

The trousers were sent and George was at church for the next three Sundays. Then he stopped coming. After two or three weeks the clergyman met him again.

"Well, George, you have no excuse for not coming to church now. Why haven't I seen you there?"

"Look here, Pastor," said George. "I know you're thinking about those trousers. I came to church three Sundays, and if you don't think I've earned the trousers, just tell me how many more Sundays I have to come to church before they're mine altogether."

Very lazy indeed—The laziest man in town got his dubious title by typewriting his prayers and taping them on his bedroom wall. When he goes to bed he points to the sheet of paper and says, 'There's my sentiments, Lord. Read 'em."

Be considerate—A minister was called out late one night to visit a man who was very ill. After he had done what he could for the man, who was at death's door, he asked the relatives why he was fetched.

"I don't think I know you," said the minister. "Haven't you got a minister of your own?"

"Yes," was the reply, "but we couldn't risk him with typhoid."

A thanksgiving—After returning from a vacation one summer, one of the members of the congregation offered this prayer, "We thank thee, Lord, for bringing our pastor and his wife back to us in safety. We know, Lord, that thou preservest both man and beast!"

There is a limit—The priest was admonishing one of his flock in an effort to make him give up drink. "I tell you, Paul," he said, "you should give it up. Whiskey is your worst enemy."

"My enemy, is it, Father?" said Paul, "Didn't you tell us just last Sunday that we should love our enemies?"

"So I did, Paul," retorted the priest, "but I didn't say you should swallow them."

Lost enthusiasm—During a marriage ceremony the groom looked extremely nervous and he got so fidgety that the best man decided to find out what was the trouble.

"What's the matter, John?" he whispered. "Have you lost the ring?"

"No," answered the groom, "the ring is safe enough, but I've lost my enthusiasm!"

A religious conscience—"You admit you are guilty then?" thundered the judge.

"I admit it, judge, I'm guilty. I stole those pants. But, your honor, there's no sin when the motive is good. I stole those pants to get baptized in."

Right kind of preaching—A man was asked by his minister, "How did you like my sermon? I've heard many good things about it from others."

"Why, preacher," said the man, "I didn't care for it at all. It was too smooth and tame for me. The kind of preaching I like is one which drives a man up into the corner of the pew and makes him think the devil is after him."

His limit—The service was unusually dull and many were nodding. The preacher stopped suddenly and said, "I refuse to preach in a dormitory or a graveyard."

Classes of members—There are usually three classes of members in each church: 1. Those who pay but do not pray or work; 2. Those who pay and pray; 3. Those who neither pay, pray nor work.

Quit when through—An elderly woman and her chauffeur attended church together. The driver would slip out when he figured the sermon was nearly over and bring the car to the door for his mistress. One Sunday he got impatient waiting in the car. Creeping down the aisle toward the mistress, he whispered to her, "Isn't he done yet?" "Done?" returned the old lady with disgust, "He's been done half an hour, but he won't stop!"

Fine efforts—It was Smith's first Sunday as usher in church, and he was a bit flustered. Turning to a lady who entered he said, "This way, madam, and I'll sew you to a sheet."

The way it seemed to him—A visitor entered the church after the sermon had begun, but soon he began to fidget. Turning to a white-haired man next to him, he whispered, "How long has he been preaching?"

"Thirty-five years in this church alone," said the old gentleman.

The stranger composed himself. "I'll wait then," he said, "he must be nearly through."

Many choice seats—A minister respectfully addressed a member of his congregation, "Mrs. Roberts, I'm pleased to see your faithful attendance every Sunday morning."

"Oh, I'm glad to come. You see, it's not every day I get a comfortable seat and so little to think about."

Quotation from Job—At a prayer meeting, testimonies were requested and a very old woman tottered to her feet. "I want to tell this blessed company that I have rheumatism in my back, I have rheumatism in my shoulders, and in my legs and in my arms, but I have been upheld and comforted by that beautiful Bible verse which says, 'Grin and bear it.'"

Shock indicated—A parson wrote to his bishop asking him to come and hold a "quiet day." The bishop declined, saying, "Your parish does not need a quiet day, it needs an earthquake."

Words out of season—A visiting preacher had finished the service and was shaking hands in the foyer. An old woman came up to him and congratulated him on the excellence of his sermon. She was moving away when another elderly woman approached who assumed the first woman had made some criticism. The second woman commented kindly, "Oh, don't mind her, she's feebleminded."

A one-day reference—A job applicant listed two ministers as references on his resume. The employer commented, "We don't work on Sundays. Don't you have a reference from someone who sees you on weekdays?"

Fire in sermons—A senior pastor was listening to the sermon of a young pastor. The speaker threw himself into the task, faithfully referring to his notes as he dabbled deep into a difficult theological subject. The young preacher concluded and asked the older pastor to criticize his sermon. "Young man, you should either put more fire into your sermons, or more sermons into your fire."

Not for awhile, at least—A man returned to his hometown after a long absence and ran into his former pastor. After mentioning various friends the man asked, "Oh, by the way, when do you expect to see Deacon Smith again?"

"Never," said the minister solemnly, "the Deacon is in heaven."

Unjust in least, unjust also in much—A man met a preacher on the street one day and began to complain of the hard times. "And don't it beat all how expensive these women are? Take my wife! One day she asks for five dollars, and pretty soon for ten dollars and the next week she wants twenty dollars."

"Well," said the preacher, "what does she do with all this money?"

"Actually, I don't know. I haven't given her any yet."

No hurry—One rainy Sunday a preacher addressed a very sparse audience. Naturally he was willing to curtail his sermon, and when he reached an appropriate point, he said, "I don't want to keep you too long."

Whereupon a voice replied, "No, go on, it's still raining."

Tombstone testimony—A preacher was talking to a man to find out the character of a deceased man whose funeral he was to officiate.

"Oh, pastor, he was a man without blame, beloved and respected by all, pure in all his thoughts, and—"

"How do you know all that?" demanded the preacher.

"I read it on his tombstone," was the reply.

A common ailment—A pastor asked a woman about her health and received the following reply: "I feel very well; but I always feel bad when I feel well, because I know I'm going to feel worse afterward."

Cut 'em short—The minister said during his sermon on Sunday morning, "In each blade of grass there is a sermon." The next day one of his flock found him mowing his yard and paused to say, "Well, preacher, I'm glad to see you engaged in cutting your sermons short."

Devils in their own hometown—From a newspaper story: Mrs. Jenny Miller gave a talk on "Personal Devils." Seventeen were present, including Mrs. Miller.

The power of will—"My husband," remarked a woman, "was a confirmed smoker with an addiction to tobacco when I married him a year ago, but today he never touches the stuff."

"Good," said her friend. "To break off a lifetime habit requires a strong will."

"That's what I've got, alright, a strong will."

Delayed repentance—A man attending a revival was encouraged to repent. He stood stubborn for a time, but finally rose and said, "Friends, I want to repent and confess, but I can't do it while the grand jury is in session."

"The Lord will forgive," shouted the revivalist.

"Yes, but he isn't on that grand jury!"

Past blessings not enough—A servant was invited to come along to church with his employers one morning. After the service the wife asked him, "How did you like our church, Jim?"

"Not much ma'am," Jim replied. "This isn't the church for me. They waste too much time reading the minutes of the previous meeting."

By-products—The preacher was talking with an old woman about religious matters. "Do you really believe, Mrs. Jones, that people are made of dust?" the preacher asked.

"Yes, sir!" The Bible says they are and I believe it."

"But what happens in wet weather, when there's nothing but mud?"

"Then I suppose they make infidels and such."

Excuses, excuses—"Good morning," said the pastor to the wife of one of his members, "is your husband home?"

"Yes, he's home, but he's in bed, pastor."

"Why didn't he come to church Sunday? You know, we must have our hearts in the right place."

"Sir," replied the wife, "his heart's all right, it's his late nights that need the work."

Hunting better pasture—"I'm sorry your husband isn't here, Mrs. Smith," said the preacher, "I'm afraid you forgot to tell him I intended to preach today on government problems."

"I didn't forget. But he said he'd stay at home and read his Bible."

Timely—"That was certainly a fine sermon," gushed an enthusiastic church member, who was an admirer of the minister. "A fine sermon, and well-timed too."

"Yes," added a less charitable eavesdropper, "it certainly was well-timed. Fully half of the congregation had their watches out."

Danger of coming late—A church member came in one morning just as the pastor was taking a collection to buy a much-needed chandelier. "Well, Brother Jones," said the preacher, "how much will you put in to help buy the chandelier?"

The old gentleman replied, "Not a cent! If we needed it, things might be different, but I dare say if we had one, there's not a soul in town who could play on it."

Necessary precaution—The usher was closing the windows one hot Sunday morning during the services when he was beckoned to the side of a young lady. "Why are you shutting those windows?" she demanded, "The air in here is suffocating now!"

"It's the minister's orders," replied the usher. "It's a breezy day outside, Miss Thomas, and we aren't going to take the chance of losing any lambs of this fold while there's a big debt overhanging this church."

Unsurpassed tact—A minister married a sweet young couple. After the ceremony the groom asked, "How much do I owe you, reverend?"

"Oh," said the minister, "Pay me whatever it's worth to you."

The young fellow looked adoringly at his bride. Then he turned to the minister and said, "I'm in your debt for life, reverend, my whole life."

Light on the Commentary—An old woman was given a set of Bible study books in order to aid her Bible study. A friend asked her if she got much help from them. The old lady replied, "The Bible certainly throws a lot of light on those books."

Some will bust—A good old woman indignantly declared, "Some church members are no good! They bust out with their religion on Sunday, and bust up on Monday."

A loyal sectarian—"Your uncle is a very religious man, I understand."

"Oh, yes! He positively hates everybody who belongs to any other church than his own."

Better believed in than practiced—The young lady said she was a firm believer in the good old Methodist doctrine of falling from grace. In fact, she sometimes practiced it.

The following admonition was addressed by a Quaker to a man who was pouring forth a volley of ill language against him:

"Have a care friend, thou mayest run thy face against my fist."

Preacher: "How did you like my sermon?"

Man: "It was like the peace and mercy of God."

Preacher: "Oh, I scarcely hoped to achieve that. How can you make such a comparison?"

Man: "Very easily. It was like the peace of God, because it passed all understanding, and, like His mercy, I thought it would have endured forever."

1st man: "Did you hear Robinson snoring in church this morning?"
2nd man: "Yes, I did. He woke me up."

Said a Baptist to a Methodist:
"I don't like your church government, it has too much machinery."
"Yes, but then you see," said the Methodist, 'it don't take near so much water to run it."

New Pastor: "What did you think of my sermon?"
Woman: "Very good indeed, sir. So instructive. We really didn't know what sin was till you came here."

Pastor: "It's terrible for a man like you to make every other word an oath."
Man: "Yes, I swear a good deal and you pray a good deal, but we don't neither of us mean nothin' by it."

1st man: "Why did your church service last so long today?"
2nd man: "Well, our preacher preaches until he hears the train whistle blow, and that confounded express was 35 minutes late!"

An emotional visitor in church hollered "Praise God! in the middle of the sermon.
Immediately one of the ushers tapped him on the shoulder and said: "You can't do that in this church, sir."

"There ought to be a special place in Heaven for ministers' wives."
Minister's wife: "Perhaps you're right, but I would much rather go with my husband."

Wife: "Did you notice the fur coat on that woman sitting in front of us at church?"
Husband: "No, I'm afraid I was dozing most of the time."
Wife: "Um! A lot of good the service did you."

1st man: "How late do you usually sleep on Sunday morning?"
2nd man: "It all depends."
1st man: "Depends on what?"
2nd man: "The length of the sermon."

Preacher: "Do you ever attend a place of worship?"
Young man: "Yes, sir, every Sunday night. I'm on my way to see her now."

An old lady in church was seen to bow whenever the name of Satan was mentioned. One day the minister met her and asked her the reason. "Well," she replied, "politeness cost nothing, and you never can tell."

Man: "I understand that you have a small congregation at your church."
Woman: "Yes, so small that every time our pastor says, 'Dearly Beloved' you feel as if you had received a proposal!"

Preacher: "The fool hath said in his heart, there is no God."
Man: "I can't say that I agree with you. I think there might be a God after all."

Preacher: "All members of this church who want to go to Heaven, stand up."
All rose except one man.
Preacher: "What! Don't you want to go to heaven?"
Man: "Not immediately."

Preacher: "We will now have a few minutes of prayer. Deacon, will you lead?"
Deacon: "'Tain't my lead, I just dealt."

Elderly lady: "What kind of Bible are you using, preacher?"
Preacher: "I'm reading from the revised version."
Elderly lady: "The King James version was good enough for St. Paul and it's good enough for me."

Trying to lie his way out, the man said: "I read the other day about how there was only seven deadly sins, and I swear to you I haven't committed one of them."
Preacher: "Which one?"

4

Don't Misspell Tithe (The Cheapskates)

Proper credit—A tight-fisted man put ten dollars in the collection plate instead of one dollar which he intended to give. Upon noticing his mistake he asked to have it back, but was refused by the old usher. "In once, in forever," the usher said. "Oh, well," grunted the miser, "I'll get credit in heaven." "No, no," replied the usher, "you'll get credit only for the dollar."

Give or take—The usher approached a parishioner and held out the box. "I never give to missions," whispered the parishioner.

"Then take something out of the box, sir," whispered the collector, "the money is for the heathen."

A narrow escape—Three tight-fisted men were in church on Sunday morning when the minister made a strong appeal for some worthy cause, hoping that everyone in the congregation would give at least five dollars. The three misers became very nervous as the collection plate neared them. Finally one of them fainted and the other two carried him out.

Cheerfulness, how measured—The boy's father had given him a dime and a quarter, telling the boy that he could put one or the other in the Sunday school collection plate. At dinner the father asked which coin had been given.

"Well, Father," responded the lad, "at first it seemed that I ought to put the quarter in the plate, but just in time I remembered the saying, 'The Lord loves a cheerful giver,' and I knew I could give the dime a great deal more cheerfully. So I put that in."

Simple faith—The minister in a small country town was noted for his ability to extract generous offerings from his close-fisted congregation, which was made up mostly of farmers. One day the young son of one of the members accidentally swallowed a quarter, much to the excitement of the rest of the family. Every method of dislodging the coin had failed and the frightened parents were about to give up when a bright thought struck the little daughter, "Oh Mama, I know how you can get it! Send for our minister, he'll get it out of him!"

Nothing but praise—"I have nothing but praise for our young pastor," the pompous Mr. Brown remarked as he left church.

"So I observed," dryly retorted the deacon who had passed the collection plate.

A wise precaution—"Mr. Grimes," said the rector to the usher on the Sunday morning before Christmas, "this morning we'd better take up the collection before the sermon."

"Why?" asked the usher.

"I mean to preach on the subject of economy," replied the rector.

One cause for thanks—The preacher was holding services in a small country church and at the conclusion he lent his hat to a member (as was the custom) to pass for contributions. The usher canvassed the congregation thoroughly, but the hat was returned to the owner empty.

The preacher looked into it, turned it upside down, and shook it vigorously. He sighed audibly. "Brethren," he said, "I sure am glad that I got my hat back."

Tardy charity—A millionaire lay dying. As he looked back on his life, he felt some remorse for the way he had lived. To the minister at his bedside he muttered weakly, "If I leave $100,000 to the church, will my salvation be assured?"

The minister answered cautiously, "I wouldn't like to give you false hope, but I think it's well worth trying."

Meeting cooled—A man asked an old preacher which subject he usually preached to his congregation. "Oh, different subjects," replied the preacher. "Sometimes I preach on love, sometimes on baptism, sometimes on heaven, and such subjects."

"Why don't you preach occasionally on the subject of contributions?"

"Well, I'll tell you, when I preach on that subject it always throws a kind of coldness over the meeting."

High financing—"The contribution this morning," said Parson Johnson, "will be for making up the deficit in your pastor's salary. The choir will now sing and will continue to sing until the full amount is collected."

Showers of greenbacks—The pastor was making an appeal for a large collection to properly decorate the church for Old Home Week. After he had made his appeal he announced the hymn, "Showers of Blessing." But he changed the words to read in this way:
There shall be showers of greenbacks
Showers of greenbacks we need.
Little dimes 'round us are falling,
But for the greenbacks we plead.

Puzzling problem—"When I look at this congregation," said the preacher, "I ask myself, 'Where are the poor?' And when I look at the collection I say to myself, 'Where are the rich?'"

Ecclesiastical dues enforced—"I can't believe I made such a mistake," Stan remarked to his wife. "I put $20 in the collection plate this morning instead of my usual $5 contribution."

The usher had noticed the mistake and in silence he allowed Stan to miss the plate for the next three Sundays. On the fourth Sunday he again ignored the plate, but the usher brought the collection round to him again and sternly said, "Your time's up now, Stan."

A remedy for spooks—A traveler, who was unable to reach an inn before nightfall, took shelter in a deserted house near the roadside. He built a fire in the fireplace and sat down to rest. Soon he heard strange noises and saw a ghost flit across the room. The traveler didn't like the idea of spending a night in a haunted house, but thought possibly he could drive the spook away. First he decided to sing a hymn, but the ghost evidently was not scared of music. Being a religious man, he tried praying loudly and fervently, but the ghost did not seem to be afraid of this either. Finally the man decided to take a collection, whereupon the ghost quickly vanished and was seen no more that night.

He was sorry—"Children, if you had two quarters, one to put in the Sunday School collection and the other your mother had given you to buy an ice cream cone, and on the way to Sunday school you should drop one of the quarters and it would roll down into a drain in the street and be lost, which one would it be?" Usually children will answer in favor of the Sunday School, but one little boy said, as he imagined his quarter disappear, "I'm sorry, Lord, but there goes your quarter."

Very bright then—PARISHIONER: "Did you see the two diamond rings my husband gave me for Christmas?"

MINISTER: "Yes, I saw them when you put that quarter in the collection plate."

Force of habit—A conductor on the Santa Fe was converted and united with the church. After he had been faithful in his religious duties for some weeks, he was asked one Sunday morning to help take the offering. He started down the aisle, and all went well until he came to a richly dressed woman. She allowed the plate to go past her, whereupon the conductor said, "Madam, if you don't pay you'll have to get off."

Promise—A little boy who became timid when left alone in his dark bedroom, was overheard by his mother to pray in his loneliness, "Oh Lord, don't let anyone hurt me, and I'll go to church next Sunday and give you some money."

Destination doubtful—"Oh, Pastor, I wish I could take my gold with me," said a dying man who was very wealthy but very selfish.

"It might melt," was the minister's consoling reply.

More than he expected—The minister arose to address his congregation. "There is a certain man among us today who is carrying on with another man's wife. Unless he puts a twenty-dollar bill in the collection, his name will be read from the pulpit.

When the collection plate came in there were 19 twenty-dollar bills and a ten-dollar bill with this note attached, "Other half on payday."

Hit at the right time—A wealthy man was in a meeting where the question of building a new church was being discussed. The wealthy man was of the opinion that churches should not be too fancy and that the old church would do for a while yet. However, he did say that he would give $500 if they decided to build. As he took his seat a piece of plaster fell from the ceiling and struck him smartly on his bald head. The man stood up again immediately and said that the need for a new church was more pressing than he had realized and that he would raise his pledge to $5000. A pious brother who had witnessed the good effect of the falling of the plaster fervently prayed, "Lord, hit him again!"

Putting on the brakes—A preacher was giving a rousing sermon for the purpose of getting a big collection. In his remarks he cried, "Brothers, this church has got to walk!" "Let her walk, Brother, let her walk," came an enthusiastic response from the amen corner. Warmed by this encouragement, the preacher yelled, "This church has got to run!" "Let her run, let her run!" came the reply. "This church has got to fly, brothers, this church has got to fly!" This eloquence brought forth the response, "Let her fly!" "And," continued the preacher, "it is going to take money to make this church fly." Then from the amen corner came the low, mournful words, "Just let her walk, Brother, just let her walk."

The decoy—A clergyman was filling in for a friend at a country parish. He was horrified when he witnessed the head usher quietly pocket a 10-dollar bill from the collection plate before presenting the plate at the altar.

After services he called the old man into the vestry and told him with some emotion that his crime had been discovered.

The usher looked puzzled for a moment. Then he suddenly beamed and said, "Oh, Pastor, you mean that old 10-dollar bill? Why, I've led off with that for the last fifteen years!"

Much more considerate—The local church was making a drive for funds, and two sisters were calling on Mr. Jones.

"I can't give anything!" exclaimed the old man. "I owe everybody in this town already."

"But don't you think you owe the Lord something, too?" asked one of the collectors.

"I'll agree that I do," replied the old man, "but he isn't pushing me like the other creditors are."

Simple solution—Betsy was given a dollar and decided to buy herself an ice cream cone.

"Why don't you give your dollar to missions?" asked the minister, who was visiting.

"I thought about that," said Betsy, "but I think I'll buy the ice cream and let the shop owner give it to missions."

All push together—"Sister Jones, I'm taking up a collection for the benefit of our worthy pastor," exclaimed one of the brethren. "You know he's leaving us to take a church in the next county, and we thought we'd get together and give him a little momentum."

With these few remarks—The pastor announced, "The choir will now sing 'I'm Glad Salvation's Free,' while the elders pass the collection plates. The congregation will please remember that while salvation is free, we have to pay the choir for singing about it. All please contribute according to your means and not your meanness."

Bad psychology—"The preacher sure used poor judgment this morning," said Matthew.

"What do you mean?" asked John.

"He preached on 'a fool and his money are soon parted' right before the collection."

Subduing power of a collection—A street preacher called a passing policeman and complained of being annoyed by certain members of his audience. He asked to have the objectionable persons removed.

"Well," said the officer thoughtfully, "it would be difficult for me to spot them; but I'll tell you what I'd do if I were you."

"What?" asked the preacher.

"Just go around with the hat."

For revenue only—"It is my painful duty," said the preacher, "to announce that Judge Jones' chickens have been mysteriously disappearing and it is my firm conviction that the ones who carried away those chickens are right here this Sunday morning. We are now going to march up to the front and lay our offerings on the table, and this collection will reveal the guilty parties."

The members marched to the front and laid an unusually large offering on the table. Without further announcements, the preacher delivered his message and was about to dismiss the audience when a man asked, "When are you going to tell us who stole those chickens?"

"Never mind, brother, never mind," said the preacher. "That story I told you is an allegory. I told you that for revenue purposes only."

Effect of music—It is said that music will make the cows give more milk. Probably this is the reason that some churches have music while taking the offering.

"What do you like the most about church, Bobby?" asked his mother.

"I like best when they pass around the money. I only got a quarter this time though."

Turning to has dad, Bobby asked, "How much did you get, Dad?"

Pastor: "Is there anyone here that wishes to pray for their failings?"

Man: "Yes, I'm a spendthrift and I throw my money around."

Pastor: "Very well, we will join in prayer for this brother, right after we pass the collection plate."

"Brothers and sisters, I have a ten dollar sermon, a twenty dollar sermon and a fifty dollar sermon. The deacons will now pass the collection plate so I will know which sermon this congregation wants to hear."

The sermon lingered and the tired little boy whispered to his mom, "If we give him the money now, will he let us leave?"

Two men were caught under a tree during a fierce thunderstorm.

1st man: "Can you pray?"

2nd man: "I don't know any prayers."

1st man: "Can you sing?"

2nd man: "I don't know any hymns."

1st man: "Well, something religious better be done mighty quick. Suppose you pass around the contribution box."

5

Miscellaneous Hoots

She was warned—A deaf but pious lady visited a small country church, armed with her ear trumpet. The elders had never seen one and viewed it with suspicion. After a short consultation one of them went up to the lady and, wagging his finger at her, whispered, "One toot and you're out!"

He could do it—This story has been applied to President Theodore Roosevelt, among others, and may be adjusted as the storyteller pleases.

After his death the energetic "Teddy" ascended to heaven. There he became a busybody and made himself a nuisance by trying to run the place. St. Peter was finally told to give T.R. the job of organizing a new choir.

"Well, I'll take the job," said Teddy. "I must have ten thousand sopranos, ten thousand altos, and ten thousand tenors. And hurry up, everything is waiting on you," he told St. Peter.

"Fine," said St. Peter, "but what about the basses?"

"Never mind about the basses," replied T.R., "I will sing bass."

Not in the book—It was at a big camp meeting and hats had been passed round to receive the collection. The preacher rose and said, "Let us sing while the hats are coming in."

The pianist, after some fumbling with the pages, turned to the minister and said, "I can't find it."

"What?" said the preacher, not understanding.

"That song 'While the Hats are Coming In.' It isn't in my book," said the pianist.

A very exclusive church—A country bumpkin wanted to join a fashionable city church, and the minister knew that his upper-crust members would never

215

allow it. Not wanting to hurt the man's feelings, the minister decided to stall, and suggested the man go home and pray over it. In a few days the bumpkin came back. "Well, what have you learned from your prayers?" asked the preacher tentatively.

"Well, sir," replied the man. "I prayed and prayed, and the good Lord said to me, 'Ronald, don't worry about that church no more. I've been tryin' to get into that church myself for the last twenty years and I ain't had no luck neither.'"

Read all about it—One lady gave the Lord the following information in her nightly prayer: "Oh Lord, You have probably read in the daily papers how Your day was desecrated again yesterday."

No hurry to go—Pastor was preaching on death and the afterlife and closed his sermon by saying, "It may be but a month longer that I shall be here, perhaps a week, or even before the close of another day, I may be gone." He had hardly sat down when a young man in the back of the vestry started the old song, "Why do you wait, dear brother, why do you tarry so long?"

Disagreement certain—"I'm afraid I'll disagree with you," remarked Jonah as the whale swallowed him.

"Perhaps," replied the whale, "but that'll be nothing compared to the way the theologians will disagree when they come to discuss this incident."

In the ranks—An enthusiastic preacher at a camp meeting had just made a powerful speech. When he got through, he went down among the congregation and asked each one to "come and join the army of the Lord."

One man answered the preacher, "I've already joined."

"Where did you join?" asked the preacher.

"In the Baptist church," was the answer.

"Why, brother," said the preacher, "you aren't in the army, you're in the navy."

Reason to be proud—The preacher had just finished a chicken dinner with one of his parish families. As he looked up out of the window a rooster strutted by. "Brother," the preacher addressed the man of the house, "that sure is a mighty proud looking rooster you have there."

"Yes, sir," replied his host. "One of his sons just entered the ministry."

Farewell—A preacher amazed his congregation one Sunday morning with this announce-ment: "This will be my last Sunday with you. I have been treated so poorly by this church and its parishioners that I have accepted the position of chaplain at the penitentiary. I will now ask the choir to stand and sing 'Meet Me There.'"

He got out—The Quaker heard a strange noise in the night and found a burglar ransacking his chickens. He took his hunting rifle and called from the front porch of the house, where he had plain sight of the intruder, "Friend, I would not do thee harm for anything in the world…but thee standest where I am about to shoot."

Just consider the source—When a minister was conducting religious services in an asylum, one of the patients cried out wildly, "Do we have to listen to this?"

The minister, surprised and confused, turned to the guard and said, "Shall I stop speaking?"

The guard replied, "No, no, go on; that won't happen again. That man has only one lucid moment every seven years. Your sermon just happened to stir him."

Something similar—"So he praised her singing, did he?"

"Yes; he said it was heavenly."

"Did he really say that?"

"Well, not exactly, but he probably meant that. He said it was unearthly."

The Lord must wait—One Sunday morning on a Naval carrier the chaplain began divine service, though the admiral was not present. "The Lord is in his holy temple," began the chaplain.

At that moment the tardy admiral appeared and interrupted the service with the admonition, "Chaplain, the Lord is not in his holy temple until the admiral is present."

Spiritual problems—A young seminary student approached his professor after class and asked if he could present a spiritual problem that was troubling him.

"It's about a lady," he nervously began. "I've asked the Lord to give me a wife to help me in my work, and it looks like he's done it. I've met a lady who's young and pretty. She can play the organ and sing. She'd make a good wife for a minister."

"What seems to be the trouble?" asked the professor. "Does she love you?"

"She says she does."

"What's your problem then? Why don't you just marry her?"

"Her husband objects."

"Then what do you want me to do?" asked the professor, trying to conceal his laughter. "Do you want me to shoot him?"

"I wouldn't ask you to go that far, professor," came the student's reply, "but I sure would like to know the most scriptural way to get rid of him."

Getting back at him—"I wonder what people will wear in heaven," said the wife.

"I suppose you will want the most expensive things, the same as here on earth," retorted the grouchy husband.

"Well, you shouldn't need to worry about that," she meekly replied, "you won't be there to pay for them."

Hardly appropriate—A zealous band of Christians were holding a jail service. The prisoners were supplied with hymnbooks and encouraged to join in the singing. A song was selected and the prisoners joined heartily in singing, "If it had not been for Jesus, I'd not be here today."

The real feeling—A notice was issued by an old farmer: "Positively no more baptizing in my pasture. Twice in the last two months my gate has been left open by Christian people and I can't afford to chase cattle all over the country just to save a few sinners."

True—A man said to his friend, who was known for being eternally optimistic, "I believe you would actually find something to admire in Satan himself."

The cheerful man replied, "Well, actually, you must admit that he has great energy and perseverance."

A religious conscience—"You admit you're guilty then?" thundered the judge.

"I do, Judge, I'm guilty. I stole them pants. But, your honor, there ain't no sin when the motive is pure. I stole them pants to get baptized in."

Noah's advice needed—A mule driver was trying to drive a mule with a wagon through a gate. The mule was being stubborn and positively refused to go through the gate.

"Need any help?" called a passerby.

"No thanks," replied the driver, "but I'd like to know how Noah got two of these stubborn cusses into the Ark!"

The place to be—The old preacher said, "I would like to see all the taverns, all the casinos, all the dance halls and everything that goes with them thrown into the river." And then closing the service he said, "Brethren, let us now sing, 'Shall We Gather at the River.'"

You can't always tell—A country editor decided to adopt the city idea of posting bulletins of important events in front of his shop. Soon after he had erected his bulletin board he was told by a local physician that Deacon Jones was seriously ill. The deacon was a man of some prominence in the community, so the editor posted a series of bulletins as follows:

10 a.m.—Deacon Jones no better.

11 a.m.—Deacon Jones has relapse.

12:30 p.m.—Deacon Jones' family has been summoned.

3:10 p.m.—Deacon Jones has died and gone to heaven.

Later in the afternoon a traveling salesman happened by, stopped to read the bulletins, and going to the board added the following:

4:10 p.m.—Great excitement in heaven. Deacon Jones has not yet arrived.

A pathetic case—A big burly man called at the rectory and when the door was opened, asked to see the rector's wife, a woman well known for her charitable impulses.

"Madam," he addressed her in a broken voice, "I wish to draw your attention to the terrible plight of a poor family in this district. The father is dead, the mother is too ill to work and the nine children are starving. They are about to be turned into the street unless someone pays their arrears in rent."

"How terrible!" exclaimed the woman. "May I ask who you are?"

The sympathetic visitor applied his handkerchief to his eyes. "I'm the land-lord," he sobbed.

Where was John?—A woman whose husband had been dead some years went to a medium, who contacted the spirit of her dead husband. "My dear John," said the widow to the spirit, "are you happy now?"

"I am very happy," John replied.

"Happier than you were on earth with me?" she asked.

"Yes," was the answer. "I am far happier now than I was on earth with you."

"Tell me, John, what's it like in heaven?"

"Heaven!" said John. "I'm not in heaven."

Good wheat always acceptable—A Presbyterian and a Baptist were arguing over their respective religions. Finally one called a neighbor who was passing by and asked his opinion as to which was the only church in which to be saved.

"Well," replied the neighbor, "my son and I have been hauling wheat to the same mill for almost forty years. There are two roads that lead to the mill. Never yet, friends, has the miller asked me which road I took, but he always asks, 'Is your wheat good?'"

No preaching—A witness was called to testify in court. The counsel for the defense said to him, "Now, sir, take the stand and tell your story like a preacher."

"No way!" roared the judge. "I'll have none of that. I want you to tell the truth!"

Hidebound—A republican US senator was speaking in his home state when he was approached by a man after the banquet. The man wanted to shake the senator's hand and said, "I have followed your record in congress, and I want to tell you that I'm praying for your success. I ask God to guard and protect you and see that you are reelected to the Senate so you can continue your activities. Why, I get so enthusiastic that I almost feel that I should vote for you myself."

"Well, if that's the way you feel about it, why shouldn't you vote for me?"

"Oh, I could never do that! I'm a Democrat!"

Not acquainted—A story is told about one of Joseph Pulitzer's reporters who had been sent to a revival meeting. In the midst of the proceedings one of the preacher's assistants bent over the young reporter and urged him to come forward and be saved.

"Oh, no thank you," was the answer. "I'm a reporter and I'm here only on business."

The revivalist replied, "But there is no business so important as the Lord's."

"Maybe not," replied the reporter, "but you don't know Mr. Pulitzer."

Full particulars in the Bible—An English nobleman owned a sprawling estate on the Thames River in England, and while he was visiting in the United States he heard that a flood had occurred in the Thames Valley. Desiring to know whether his estate had sustained any flood damage, he cabled his eldest son, "Send information about the flood."

At the time his son happened to be away in Scotland and had heard nothing about the flood in England. When his father's cable was forwarded to him, he could make neither head nor tail of the request. He eventually came to the conclusion that it was some sort of joke on his father's part, so he cabled back to the United States, "Look in the Book of Genesis."

Not much help—A minister received a hurry-up call to conduct a funeral. The dear departed was a complete stranger to him, and after the service was well under way the preacher realized that he didn't know the gender of the deceased in the sealed casket. The name, unfortunately, was one of those tricky ones that may be used for either male or female. In a cold sweat the minister proceeded as diplomatically as possible, avoiding words like "he" or "she." Finally he came to a point where he simply had to know. So calling on the choir to sing, he beckoned to a nearby mourner, pointed to the casket and whispered, "Brother or sister?"

Back came the answer, "Neither; a cousin."

Cooperation—Sir Wilfred Grenfell once fitted an artificial leg on a woman in Labrador. He said, "When I, an Episcopalian, took that Presbyterian-made leg, given me by a Methodist woman in a Congregational church back to Labrador, and fitted it on my Roman Catholic friend, it enabled her to walk perfectly. Let us be merciful too, even in discussing our religious convictions."

That much certain—Young men going to the big city to carve out a career are usually more concerned with their comforts than their morals. A lad from the country applied to an employment agency and was offered a job at $150 a week.

"But," the boy protested, "can I lead a good Christian life in the city on $150 a week?"

"Believe me," was the reply, "that's the only kind of life you can lead."

Taken literally—The young wife wired her friend from the maternity ward of the hospital: "Isaiah 9:6." (*The verse reads, "Unto us a son is given."*)

The friend relayed the news to her neighbor, "Margaret has a boy weighing nine pounds six ounces and they have named him Isaiah."

Needed his touch—A successful businessman's funeral was held on a terribly hot day, and several friends and associates delivered long eulogies. A weary mourner turned to his neighbor, "Did you know him well?"

"Oh, very well. He was a remarkable man."

"Yes, he was a smart fellow. If he'd been running his funeral it would have been over in half an hour."

Why she sang the hymn—A preacher was visiting a household where, quite early one morning, he was awakened by a beautiful voice singing "Abide With Me." The preacher was impressed at the piety of the woman to do her tasks early in the morning singing such a noble hymn. At breakfast he spoke to the cook about her lovely serenade, and told her how pleased he was.

"Goodness!" she exclaimed, blushing. "That's the hymn I boil eggs by; three verses for soft and five for hard."

Outward bound—It happened one day that a New York journal transposed the headings of its obituary column and the marine and shipping news column which had chanced to fall on the same page. As a result a number of respected and deceased citizens were listed under the disconcerting heading, "Passed Through Hell Gate Today."

Too vivid—The criminal was about to be executed, and the sheriff was adjusting the black cap. The singers started the song, "Blest be the Tie that Binds."

"Hold on a minute," said the condemned man, "stop the singers. That song is too appropriate."

Very close—"Mama, I never see a picture of an angel with a beard or mustache. Don't men go to heaven?"

"Yes, dear, but it's always by a close shave."

The sheep and the goats—The soldiers marched to the church and halted in the square outside. One wing of the building was undergoing repairs, so there was room for only about half the regiment.

"Sergeant," ordered the captain, "tell the men who don't want to go to church to fall out." A large number quickly fell out.

"Now, Sergeant," continued the captain, "dismiss all the men who did not fall out and march the others in—they need it most."

Prolongation—An elder, while baptizing converts at a revival meeting, advanced with a wiry, sharp-eyed old chap into the water. He asked the usual question, whether there was any reason why the ordinance of baptism should not be administered.

After a pause a tall, powerful-looking man, who was watching quietly, remarked, "Elder, I don't want to interfere in your business, but I want to say that this is an old sinner you've got hold of and that one dip won't do him any good; you'll have to anchor him out in the deep water overnight."

Hard job—A man planning to make a business trip to Washington, DC, decided to take his young son along. After his business was concluded, the father took his boy to many historic and politically interesting sites. They ended their tour in the gallery of the Senate. Noticing a man on the Senate floor clothed in black, the boy asked, "Who is that, Daddy?"

The father whispered, "That man is the chaplain of the Senate."

"Does he pray for the Senate?" persisted the boy.

"No," replied the father, raising his eyes heavenward, "he comes in, looks at the senators, and then prays for the country."

Quite a difference—The Georgia convert was about to be baptized, but was afraid to get into the water, saying, "Brother William, there's alligators in this here stream."

"Nonsense!" said Brother William, "Anyway, didn't it turn out all right with Jonah after he was swallowed by the whale?"

"Yes," replied the convert, "but a Georgia alligator is much tougher than a whale, and he's got less conscience. After he swallows you, he goes to sleep and forgets all about you."

Bible facts worth knowing—The Bible contains 3,566,480 letters, 810,687 words, 31,175 verses, 1189 chapters and 66 books.

The longest chapter is Psalm 119.

The shortest chapter is Psalm 117.

The verse that is the halfway point is Psalm 118:8.

The longest name is in the 8th chapter of Isaiah.

The word "and" occurs 46,627 times; the word "Lord" 1855 times.

The 37th chapter of Isaiah and the 19th chapter of II Kings are alike.

The longest verse in the Bible is Esther 8:9 and the shortest verse is John 11:35.

The name of God is not mentioned in the book of Esther.

The model prayer is in the 17th chapter of John.

The 13th chapter of I Corinthians is the chapter on Christian love and is very helpful.

Going slow—Two men were adrift in an open boat and it looked bad for them. Finally one of them, frightened, began to pray.

"Oh, Lord," he prayed, "I've broken most of the commandments. I've been a hard drinker, but if my life is spared now, I'll promise to never again—"

"Wait a minute, Pete," interrupted his friend, "don't go too fast. I think I see a sail."

Uneasy—The morning sun shone brightly and the dew was still on the grass. "Ah, this is the weather that makes things spring up," remarked a passer-by casually to an old man seated on a bench in the churchyard.

"Hush!" replied the old man. "I've got three wives buried here."

Private property—I was staying one night in a country inn where an earthquake occurred. There was a preacher staying at the inn also. All at once the house began to shake, the windows began to rattle, and the plaster fell. The owner got very upset and began to swear. The preacher said, "Be calm; the Lord made this old world and he can shake it if he likes." The owner replied, "Yes, but he didn't make this old house, and he'd better leave it alone."

Well-meant, anyhow—A notice in a church bulletin read: "I take this opportunity to express my appreciation for cards, calls, flowers and other remembrances while recup-erating from my many friends."

Sure thing—"I must confess," remarked Mrs. Crabbe, "I don't believe there ever was a perfect man."

"Well," replied Mr. Crabbe, "Adam would have been, I suppose, if Eve had only been made first."

"How do you mean?"

"She could have bossed the job of making Adam."

Long on the Fourth Commandment but short on the Ninth—Mrs. Higgins was deeply shocked when neighbors called on Sunday to borrow a rug beater.

"What!" she exclaimed to her husband. "Beating rugs on Sunday! Not with my beater. Tell them we don't have one."

Strange, strange—A clergyman was preaching to the residents of a psychiatric hospital. During his sermon he noticed that one of the patients paid the closest attention, his eyes riveted upon the preacher's face, his body bent eagerly forward. Such interest was very flattering. After the service the speaker noticed that the man spoke to the superintendent, so as soon as possible the preacher inquired, "Did that man speak to you about my sermon?"

"Yes."

"Would you mind telling me what he said?"

The superintendent tried to sidestep, but the preacher insisted. "Well," he said at last, "what the man said was, 'Just think, he's out and I'm in.'"

And it was—A minister who guarded his morning study hour very carefully told the new maid that under no circumstances were visitors to be admitted—except, of course, in cases of life and death. Half an hour later the maid knocked at the door.

"I thought I told you—," the minister began.

"Yes, I told him," she replied, "but he says it is a question of life and death."

So he went downstairs and found the visitor was an insurance agent.

Questionable benefits—a man who had lost one of his legs in an accident came to a faith healer. The priest was requested to pray for the unfortunate man that his leg might be restored.

This was quite a big order for the faith healer. Taking the man aside he said, "Now, you know the Lord will restore your leg in answer to my prayers, but you should consider the consequences. You would be all right for this world, but when you get to heaven you would be burdened throughout eternity with three legs."

Revoking to wrath—A preacher was asked if the man who took tuba lessons on Sunday would go to heaven. The pastor replied, "I don't see why not, but I doubt whether his neighbor would."

Not today—A number of visitors were being shown around the psychiatric hospital by an employee. "You see that man over there? He thinks he is the Lord."

One of the visitors then asked the patient whether he really made the earth in six days.

The patient looked at him contemptuously, and said as he walked away, "I'm not in the mood to talk shop!"

The place for him—A young woman smilingly told her beau that she was going to give her entire fortune to missionaries. Slowly unwinding from her embrace, he stood and went to the door.

"Are you going already?" she asked in surprise.

"Yes," he replied, "I am going…I am going to be…a missionary."

Partaker of the deed—The son of a pious deacon brought home on the Sabbath a string of nice fish that he had caught that day. The pastor was visiting the home and thought it a good time to impress upon his deacon the importance of Sabbath observance and family training.

"Don't you realize that it is wrong to allow your son to go fishing on the Sabbath?" asked the pastor.

"Oh, yes," said the deacon.

"Aren't you going to punish your boy for this?"

"Yes, indeed," said the deacon, "but I thought I would let him clean the fish first."

Modified King James Version—Not far off the boulevard between Los Angeles and San Diego are some quaint towns, and one of them has a unique garage. At one time it was a church, but now a double door has been cut through the side and the vestibule at the front is used for an office. But the blend of old and new affords a laugh to every traveler who stops there, for over the door, weather-beaten but still readable, is a scripture quotation that goes: "Behold, I have set before you an open door." And on the panel below the mechanic has inscribed in red paint, "Positively no admittance."

The Sabbath—Randy was performing some mysterious carpentry job at the bottom of his garden one Sunday and he was making the most fearful racket with his hammering. His good wife came to the door. "What's the matter with you?" she cried. "You must not work on the Sabbath, making such a clatter! What'll the neighbors think?"

"Never mind the neighbors!" replied Randy shortly, "I must get my wheelbarrow mended."

"It's very wrong to hammer on the Sabbath," insisted his wife. "Why can't you use screws?"

He knew—YOUNG FATHER: "Pastor, in your sermon this morning you spoke of a baby's being a new wave on the ocean of life."

MINISTER: "That's right."

YOUNG FATHER: "Don't you think it would have been nearer the truth to say he is a 'fresh squall'?"

Stop signals—There is a little church which a man and his little dog attend. The man goes inside to worship and the dog lies outside to wait. If, however, the sermon lasts longer than twenty minutes, the dog puts his head inside the church door and looks up the aisle toward the preacher. It is said that this dog is a great favorite with the congregation.

Good day to do it—The architect's new employee was found by his pious boss on Sunday busily at work on plans for a large commercial building. He told his assistant that it was the practice of the office to leave off all Sunday work, and he requested that the rule be observed by all employees.

A short time afterward the assistant happened to find his boss at work on a Sunday. "You do not seem to observe your own Sunday rules," complained the assistant.

"Well, you see, this is different. I'm doing church work," he said. "I'm working on these church plans."

Diagnosis—Why do more people become sick on Wednesday than any other day of the week? The doctors finally agreed that it was because the churches usually held their prayer meetings on Wednesday evenings.

One short—The engines on the airplane suddenly missed and stopped. The pilot, looking as brave as possible, walked back among the passengers and asked, "Is there anyone here who knows how to pray?"

"I do, sir," volunteered a minister.

"Fine," said the pilot, "you go ahead and pray while the rest of us strap on these parachutes. There's one short."

Horrific—A minister was invited to dinner. During the meal he was surprised to hear the little daughter of the house state that a person must be brave these days to go to church.

"Why do you say that?" asked the minister.

"I heard Papa tell Mama that last Sunday there was a big gun in the pulpit, the choir murdered the anthem, and the organist drowned the choir."

Brief prayer—Little Erin objected strongly when her mother suggested that she repeat three times a new prayer she wanted her to memorize. "I don't want to say such long prayers," the little girl cried. "I want to say a nice short one like Nanny does."

"What kind does Nanny say?" asked her mother.

"She just says, 'Oh, Lord, why do I have to get up?'"

Speaking plainly—The minister trudged his way to the church one blizzarding morning, but found no one present except the janitor. They stood near the furnace warming them-selves for some time. Finally the minister remarked, "Ralph, it looks like no one is coming out today except you and me."

"Well," said Ralph, "I guess you and I wouldn't be here if we weren't paid for it."

Definition—A student in comparative religions wrote on his test paper: "The Christians may have only one wife. This is called monotony."

A bargain—A new clergyman in town sought the services of the best local physician, a man who seldom attended church. The medical treatment was going to be rather pro-longed, and the young pastor, worried over the expense, spoke to the doctor about his bill.

"I'll tell you what I'll do, Pastor," said the doctor. "I hear you're a pretty good preacher and you seem to think I'm a fair doctor. We'll make a bargain. I'll do all

I can to keep you out of heaven, and you do all you can to keep me out of the other place, and it won't cost either of us a cent."

Answered—A man received the following note from his actor son who had joined a touring company: "I am a great success. Will you send me $25 to pay the landlady? Your devoted son, Alan.

P.S. Since writing this letter, I am ashamed to ask you for money, so I ran after the postman and tried to get it back. I pray it does not reach you."

The son was surprised when he received this reply: "Dear Alan, Your prayer was answered. The letter did not reach me."

Playing safe—Standing at the grave of her recently departed husband, the widow said, "If you're where I think you aren't, you pray for me; but if you're where I think you are, don't mention my name."

Overdoing it—HOSTESS (to clergyman): "I've invited my neighbors to dinner at seven to meet you, but they may be a little late. I think we should give them a half hour's grace."

CLERGYMAN: "Well, now, of course I'm devout and all that, but don't you think that would be overdoing it a bit?"

In baseball terms—Two men were discussing baseball in the Bible. One made the following speech: "Eve stole first. Adam got out at the Garden of Eden; David struck out Goliath; the prodigal son made a home run. Moses shut out the Egyptians at the Red Sea."

Prayer refused—The patient was on the operating table. "Your minister is here. Do you want to see him before we begin the operation?" asked the surgeon.

"No, sir," replied the patient, "I do not want to be opened with prayer."

History—"What did the Puritans come to this country for?" asked a Massachusetts teacher.

"To worship in their own way and make other people do the same," was the reply.

White elephant—The following notice appeared in a small town newspaper: "Next Wednesday evening the Ladies' Aid will hold a rummage sale at the Methodist Church. Good chance to get rid of anything not worth keeping, but too good to throw away. Bring along your husbands."

More knee work needed—A marble-cutter was working on his knees changing a stone into a statue. A minister passing by watched the worker for awhile. "I wish that I could deal such clanging blows upon stony hearts," commented the minister.

"Maybe you could," replied the workman, "if you worked more on your knees."

Not to worry—He was a wise man who said he didn't have time to worry. In the daytime he was too busy and at night he was too sleepy.

Censorious—An old tenant on Queen Victoria's Balmoral estate was greatly concerned when the Queen went driving Sunday afternoons. She even brought up her concerns to the Queen, who smiled and said to the old woman, "The New Testament tells us distinctly that the Sabbath was made for man."

"Yes," said the woman severely, "I know it does; and I think none the more of the New Testament for that."

Treated like a minister—Once a manager asked a friend if he had ever been taken for a minister. "No," was his reply, "but I've been treated like one." "How was that?" "I kept waiting for my salary six or seven months."

Perseverance defined—A preacher when asked to define "perseverance" said, "It means, firstly, to take hold; secondly, to hold on; thirdly and lastly, to never let go."

War in heaven—Soon after the death of her wealthy husband the widow erected a monument to his memory, bearing this inscription: REST IN PEACE. On probation of the will, however, she discovered for some reason the husband had not included her among the beneficiaries.

The widow then had the inscription modified by adding the following words: TILL I COME.

Quite a stranger—"Tomorrow afternoon," said the minister to his congregation, "the funeral of Mr. James Garren will be held at this church. I shall make a funeral address, and the man himself will be here for the first time in twenty years."

How sects grow—Probably many religious sects rest on trivial differences in belief. Two men, prominent in church work, were traveling through a sparsely settled community when they noticed two churches immediately opposite each other. Stopping a native, they asked why there were two churches for so few people.

"It's like this," the native replied. "The church members on the right believe that Eve tempted Adam; and the ones on the left believe that Adam was a rascal from the beginning."

Rated himself high—A judge detected a witness' hand hovering above the Bible instead of touching it as ordered. His Honor exclaimed sternly, "You may think to deceive God, sir, but you can't deceive me."

Tracts that track people—A minister gave a man a tract and several days later asked him what he thought of it. "Oh, it does my soul good! I never knew before why they call them tracts, but when I read that little book it tracked me this way and that; when I go out in the barn, it tracks me there, when I come in the house, it tracks me there. It tracks me everywhere I go."

Her marital creed—Mrs. Worth had just learned that her maid, at the age of seventy, had married for the fourth time.

The maid smiled at the congratulations and said, "Just as often as the Lord takes 'em, so will I."

Not headed for the stars—A boat on the St. Louis River in Florida ran into a heavy fog and stopped. An impatient passenger asked the captain, "Why don't you go on?"

"Don't you see the fog?" asked the captain.

"Yes, but I see the stars, too, they are shining."

"So they are," replied the captain. "But unless the boiler bursts, we are not going in that direction."

Step by step—If the elevator to heaven is not running, climb the stairs.

Sitting on the lid—An old Quaker was very conscientious about saying unkind things about his neighbors. On one occasion a neighbor started a rumor about him, which greatly disturbed the old Quaker. He felt it his Christian duty to go and tell him of his fault. This, however, did not help, as each became very angry, and the man who started the rumor spoke harshly and rudely to his Quaker neighbor. The Quaker stood it as long as he could then said, "I will not call thee a liar. But if the governor should come down here hunting the biggest liar in the country, I would tell thee that the governor wished to see thee!"

Argument without knowledge—A religious argument arose between two men who knew little about the Bible. One offered, in order to prove the other's ignorance, to wager that he could not repeat the Lord's prayer. The other accepted the challenge and said, "Now I lay me down to sleep..." When the prayer was over the other man said, "Dang, I was sure you wouldn't know it," and paid the bet.

Sing it—Whenever an argument arose amongst the children of the house, the mother would call to them, "Sing it, sing it." Often the song began, "You cheated, you cheated," or "I hate you, I hate you!" But quickly it changed to smiles and laughter that it became a family proverb, "Never say what you cannot sing."

The drawbacks of religion—A woman consulted a lawyer, saying she wanted a divorce.

"On what grounds," asked the lawyer.

"That man's gotten religion and we haven't seen a chicken on the table for over two weeks."

Sabbath desecration—One Sunday a lady took her maid with her to church for the first time. After church the mistress asked her if she liked the service.

"Yes, ma'am," responded the girl. "It was very nice."

"And wasn't the singing lovely?"

"Oh, yes," replied the girl, "it was. But don't you think it's an awful way to spend the Sabbath?"

A good job hinders many—A cook was employed on Mr. Johnson's cruise ship. One summer they landed at a place where a camp meeting was in full blast. The cook was very interested and took a front seat.

Near the close of the meeting one of the brethren went about among the people exhorting them to "go forward." Coming to the cook, he asked, "My friend, don't you want to work for Jesus?"

"Oh, no thank you," said the cook, "I've got a good job with Johnson."

Faith not equal to the occasion—Father and son were taking a walk when they came near a yard with a large dog barking viciously. The boy was afraid the dog's chain would break and wanted to turn back for home. The father gently scolded him, reminding that Jesus would protect them, but this didn't make the boy any braver.

"Papa," he said, "you're a Christian and so am I, but the dog doesn't know that!"

Sing or perform—An old farmer and his wife lived near the village church. One warm Sunday evening, while they sat dozing on the porch, the crickets set up a loud chirping. "I just love to hear that chirpin' noise," said the old man drowsily, and soon he was fast asleep in his chair.

Soon after the church choir broke into a beautiful chant. "Just listen to that," exclaimed his wife, "isn't that beautiful?"

"Yes," murmured the farmer sleepily, "they do it with their hind legs."

Saloon helped one business—"If any man here," shouted the temperance speaker, "can name an honest business that has been helped by the saloon I will spend the rest of my life working for the liquor people."

A man in the audience arose. "I consider my business honest," he said, "and it has been helped by the saloon."

"What is your business?" yelled the orator.

The man responded, "I'm an undertaker."

Mixed saints—A member of the legislature was making a speech on some momentous question and in concluding said, "In the words of Daniel Webster, who wrote the dictionary, 'Give me liberty or give me death.'" One of his colleagues pulled at his coat and whispered, "Daniel Webster didn't write the dictionary, it was Noah." "Noah nothing," replied the speaker. "Noah built the ark."

Is it possible?—Note to preachers: Every service is just as long as it seems.

A shipwrecked traveler was washed up on a small island: He was terrified at the thought of cannibals and discovering a thin wisp of smoke about the scrub, he crawled toward it fearfully, in apprehension that it might be from the campfire of savages. But as he came close, a voice rang out sharply.

"Why in the hell did you play that card?"

The castaway, already on his knees, raised his hands in devout thanksgiving and said: "Thank God! They are Christians!"

At the request of his wife, the husband opened a can of peaches. When he finally reappeared, the wife asked demurely:

"What did you use to open that can?"

"Can opener, of course," the husband grunted. "What did you think I opened it with?"

Wife: "From the language I heard, I thought perhaps you were opening it with prayer."

Within limits—
O Lord, I thank Thee for the love
    That makes my life so bright,
For this I praise Thee Sabbath morn—
    But not on Sunday night.

I love to hear our pastor speak,
    His views are sound and right,
They feed my soul on Sabbath morn—
    But not on Sunday night.

At ten A.M. I stroll to church
    In Sunday clothes quite right,
But, Lord, I crave my easy chair
    And slippers Sunday night.

Remember, send your stories for future books!
Ken Alley, PO Box 397 York, Ne 68467
alleykat51@hotmail.com

0-595-29728-5